Gabit Sanford

Values in Translation

Stanford Studies in Human Rights

Values in Translation

Human Rights and the Culture
of the World Bank

Galit A. Sarfaty

Stanford University Press
Stanford, California

Stanford University Press
Stanford, California

Printed in the United States of America on acid-free, archival-quality paper

Library of Congress Cataloging-in-Publication Data

Sarfaty, Galit A., 1978- author.
  Values in translation : human rights and the culture of the World Bank / Galit A. Sarfaty.
    pages cm --(Stanford studies in human rights)
  Includes bibliographical references and index.
    ISBN 978-0-8047-6351-6 (cloth : alk. paper)--ISBN 978-0-8047-6352-3 (pbk. : alk. paper)
    1. Human rights. 2. World Bank. I. Title. II. Series: Stanford studies in human rights.
  K3240.S2655 2012
  332.1'532--dc23   2012007604

Typeset by Bruce Lundquist in 10/14 Minion Pro

To Adam

Contents

Foreword

IN *VALUES IN TRANSLATION*, anthropologist and legal scholar Galit Sarfaty pulls back the curtain to reveal a surprising conflict within one of the world's most consequential and controversial institutions. As the principal international institution of market based economic development in the postwar period, the World Bank is formally charged to reduce poverty by providing credit to countries in exchange for commitments to reform and restructure national political economies, to bring them into line with the Bank's expectations about efficiencies and the role of the state. As Sarfaty explains, this mission attracts economists, finance specialists, lawyers, and policy makers who understand the need for international institutions; however, many of them also believe that what she calls "economic rationality" should form the epistemological foundation for decision making.

But the Bank became a target for a wide range of critique and political analysis, especially over the last twenty years, and reluctance to acknowledge the broader political consequences of its lending practices was seen by many critics as a strategy to allow dominant nation-states such as the United States (which holds the largest voting bloc within the Bank and traditionally controls the presidency) to use the Bank to promote policies that ultimately reinforce the position of the world's biggest national economies. Partly as a response to this critique, the Bank expanded its mandate to incorporate formerly excluded "political" programs that would broaden the means through which its formal goal of poverty reduction could be accomplished. These included now-well-known initiatives under the rubrics of "good governance" and "anticorruption," which brought the Bank's programming into areas of national politics and law that had historically been understood to be outside the scope of its Articles of Agreement. As Sarfaty argues, exclusion of political activities by the Bank had been seen, since the Bank's founding in 1944, as necessary to allay fears on the part of potential client countries—many with fragile or problematic political regimes—that the Bank would not interfere with their sovereignty. Moreover, the formally apolitical nature of the Bank proved to be useful for major donor countries that did not want their financial contributions to be seen as politically instrumental (however much they, in fact, were).

Expansion of Bank projects into political domains unleashed forces, both internal to the Bank and outside it, that have so far only marginally changed the institutional ethos and what might be called a sense of organizational self. But even these small shifts mark an important moment in the relationship between the Bank and its client countries and, perhaps even more far-reaching, between the Bank and the largely well-meaning technocrats who oversee day-to-day operations. It is the latter group that forms the basis for Sarfaty's study. She was given an unprecedented level of access to people and policy making within the Bank itself in order to conduct ethnographic research into the Bank's organizational culture and efforts by a small cadre of Bank employees (mostly lawyers) who have been struggling to find ways to make a concern with human rights relevant to Bank projects and policy making. What results is a powerful inside view of the Bank that holds out at least the possibility of larger shifts to come in the organizational mission, while also revealing the hidden costs to human rights that would result from such deeper institutional changes.

As Sarfaty explains, these internal Bank activists face long odds. On the one hand, human rights have been ignored in at least three ways: (1) the Bank does not consider the impact of lending projects on the human rights of people in client countries, (2) it does not require client countries to comply with international treaty obligations as a prerequisite for development assistance, and (3) it does not suspend projects when client countries are suspected of violating the human rights of their citizens. On the other hand, these activists must make their case within the dominant discursive paradigm of the Bank, in which policy is translated in terms of cost-benefit economic theory. In this way, *Values in Translation* is not just a study of an important conflict within the World Bank but an analysis of the broader struggle that this conflict represents: the neo-Cold War struggle between two dominant shaping logics of the post-Cold War, the logic of rational and efficient markets and the logic of what Sarfaty calls "social contract liberalism." What Sarfaty discovers about the course of this struggle as it plays out within the World Bank provides a necessary and essential starting point for those who have called for human rights reforms within international institutions.

Mark Goodale
Series Editor
Stanford Studies in Human Rights

Acknowledgments

THIS BOOK has greatly benefited from discussions and comments from many individuals and the support of various institutions. I couldn't have conducted this study without the generous time of the World Bank staff, whom I learned from tremendously and whose work I continue to respect and admire. I would like to thank Jacob Levy, Joseph Masco, and Sally Engle Merry for their tireless support and insightful comments that have significantly strengthened this manuscript. I am especially grateful to John Comaroff for his mentorship and inspiration throughout the years and his extraordinary editing and feedback on countless drafts. I would also like to thank these individuals for their guidance and extensive feedback during the phases of this project: Alfred Aman, Arthur Applbaum, Daniel Bradlow, Rachel Brewster, Kamari Clarke, Cosette Creamer, Adrian Di Giovanni, Mark Goodale, Ryan Goodman, Oona Hathaway, Laurence Helfer, Harold Hongju Koh, Claudio Lomnitz, Paul McDonald, Bronwen Morgan, Martha Nussbaum, Robert Post, Mindy Roseman, Cora True-Frost, and David Wilkins. The staff at Stanford University Press, particularly executive editor Kate Wahl, and the external reviewers were extremely helpful and supportive during the writing and production of the book. Finally, I thank my family and especially my husband, Adam Saunders, for their continued love and support.

I have received invaluable feedback from participants at Brown University, Harvard Business School, Harvard Law School, Hebrew University of Jerusalem Faculty of Law, McGill University's anthropology department, Temple Law School, the University of Pennsylvania anthropology department, and the University of Toronto Faculty of Law, as well as at conferences of the American Anthropological Association, the American Society of International Law, the Conference on Empirical Legal Studies, and the

Law and Society Association. I gratefully acknowledge generous financial support for this research from the National Science Foundation's Cultural Anthropology Program and Law and Social Sciences Program (grant no. 0513960), Social Science Research Council, Woodrow Wilson Foundation, and Andrew W. Mellon Foundation. The Wharton School, the American Academy of Arts and Sciences, Harvard University's Edmond J. Safra Center for Ethics, and Harvard Law School's Human Rights Program and Program on the Legal Profession served as enriching and stimulating environments as I wrote up my manuscript.

Parts of this book were adapted from earlier published articles and book chapters: "Why Culture Matters in International Institutions: The Marginality of Human Rights at the World Bank," *American Journal of International Law*, 2009, 103:647–83; "Measuring Justice: Internal Conflict over the World Bank's Empirical Approach to Human Rights," in *Mirrors of Justice: Law and Power in the Post–Cold War Era*, pp. 131–46 (Kamari Clarke and Mark Goodale, eds., Cambridge University Press, 2009); "Doing Good Business or Just Doing Good: Competing Human Rights Frameworks at the World Bank," in *The Intersection of Rights and Regulation: New Directions in Sociolegal Scholarship*, pp. 93–106 (Bronwen Morgan, ed., Ashgate Press, 2007); and "The World Bank and the Internalization of Indigenous Rights Norms," *Yale Law Journal*, 2005, 114:1791–1818.

Values in Translation

NTERNATIONAL ORGANIZATIONS (IOs) have emerged as significant actors in global governance, whether they are overseeing monetary policy, setting trade or labor standards, or resolving a humanitarian crisis. They often execute international agreements between states and markedly influence domestic law, which makes it important to analyze how international institutions behave and make policy. Conducting an ethnographic analysis of the internal dynamics of IOs, including their formal and informal norms, incentive systems, and decision-making processes, can usefully aid in understanding the interactions among legal, social, ethical, and political norms and the reasons certain policies and laws are adopted and internalized. Human rights is a particularly challenging policy agenda to institutionalize, given its universalist claims and seemingly nonnegotiable principles. The global yet politically contested nature of human rights makes it a fascinating lens to understand how global institutions operate. This book analyzes the organizational culture of one particularly powerful international institution—the World Bank (the Bank)—and explores why the Bank has not adopted a human rights policy or agenda.

Established on July 1, 1944, the Bank has become the largest lender to developing countries, lending more than $20 billion per year.[1] The World Bank Group, one of the United Nations' specialized agencies, consists of five closely associated institutions that are governed by member countries. The Bank is probably the most well-known symbol of economic globalization, capitalism, and Western imperialism. Its more than ten thousand employees (including economists, sociologists, lawyers, and engineers, among others) are engaged in the Bank's official mission of poverty reduction, which it carries out primarily through development lending. Its legitimacy depends on fulfillment of the mission, which is inextricably linked to human rights. The institution may be implicated in human rights in at least three possible activities: the Bank's direct or indirect violation of human rights through its projects (e.g., forcible displacement of indigenous peoples resulting from a Bank-financed dam project), its lending of money to governments that have committed gross and systemic human rights violations, and its reluctance to directly support human rights in its activities. If the Bank finances projects that hinder the rights of vulnerable peoples or channels investments to state governments that do so, it harms its reputation and relevance as a global leader in fighting poverty and compromises the development outcomes of its projects.

Although the institution has adopted various social and environmental policies and works on issues as diverse as judicial reform, health, and infrastructure, it has not instituted any overarching operational policy on human rights. Despite the Bank's rhetoric that protecting human rights is critical for development, its employees do not systematically incorporate human rights concerns into their everyday decision making or consistently take them into consideration in lending; incorporation of human rights is ad hoc and at their discretion. In addition, many employees consider it taboo to discuss human rights in everyday conversation and to include such references in their project documents.[2] The marginality of human rights in official policy stands in contrast to the Bank's rhetoric in official reports and public speeches given by its leadership, which have supported human rights (see World Bank 1998; Alston and Robinson 2005).

What do I mean by saying that human rights is a marginal issue within the Bank? In general, I mean that the Bank maintains no comprehensive or consistent approach at the policy and operational levels. In more specific terms, the marginality of human rights at the Bank entails resisting adoption of such provisions as (1) a staff policy to mitigate the impact of its projects on human rights; (2) a requirement to consider countries' obligations under international human rights law when Bank employees engage in country dialogues or draft Country Assistance Strategies;[3] and (3) guidelines on when it would suspend operations because of human rights violations. In contrast, other multilateral development agencies have instituted human-rights-based programming; for instance, the United Nations Development Programme has conducted country program reviews based on human rights criteria, and bilateral aid agencies, such as those of Denmark (DANIDA), Sweden (SIDA), and the United Kingdom (DFID), have adopted human rights approaches in their strategies and policies.

Whether and how the Bank should adopt human rights has been discussed at length by academics and civil society advocates (see, e.g., Darrow 2003; Skogly 2001). This literature focuses primarily on legal arguments for binding the Bank and its member countries to international human rights obligations. It does not investigate the internal workings of the bureaucracy so as to understand *why* the Bank has yet to adopt and internalize human rights norms. I argue that legal and political obstacles do not fully explain this phenomenon; what has been missing from existing explanations is an anthropological analysis of the Bank's organizational culture that would uncover internal obstacles to the adoption of human rights norms. This study offers an ethnographic analysis of the Bank's organizational culture that is based on extensive field research at the institution itself, including personal interviews, participant observation, and analysis of Bank documents.

The Dilemma of Human Rights in the World Bank

The World Bank has had a problematic relationship with human rights since its founding in 1944. Because it was created in the aftermath of World War II as the International Bank for Reconstruction and Development, one would expect that human rights to be part of the Bank's work program from its inception. However, the Bank has interpreted human rights as beyond its mandate under the Articles of Agreement, which prohibit interference in the political affairs of members (Art. IV, Sec. 10) and limit to nonpolitical considerations those factors that the Bank can consider in granting loans (Art. III, Sec. 5(b)). The reason for this interpretation lies in the cultural history of the institution.

The Bank's apolitical, technical image was historically shaped by the need to attract clients (who did not want the Bank to encroach upon their fragile sovereignty) and by the agendas of donor countries (who wanted to pursue their foreign policy goals through a seemingly neutral organization; Weaver 2008). Hiding behind the Articles of Agreement, it has attempted to mask the true political intents and ideological practices, including maintaining relations of domination (Mosse 2004a) and entrenching donor interests and goals (specifically, creation of ideal conditions for international finance and investment). Yet its interventionist techniques, under the guise of poverty alleviation and "development," have become a form of neocolonialism and cultural imperialism, where "local ownership" of development strategies is merely a myth that conceals donor-recipient inequalities.

Subject to pressure to increase lending so as to legitimate its purpose and existence, in the 1960s and 1970s the Bank shifted the focus from postwar reconstruction to poverty alleviation and expanded the sectoral portfolio to include health, education, rural development, and agriculture. The shift to a mission of poverty reduction enabled the Bank to assert a new justification for existence, further strengthen its power, and expand its reach into new domains of social intervention. As Balakrishnan Rajagopal argues, "The development apparatus is not a machine for the elimination of poverty, which incidentally leads to increasing international bureaucracy; rather development is principally a machine for expanding the bureaucratization of the international sphere, which takes 'poverty' as its incidental point of entry" (Rajagopal 2003, 112).

Since the 1970s, the Bank has reinterpreted its mandate to gradually incorporate issues previously regarded as "political" into the work program, albeit in a supposedly depoliticized form by connecting them to economic growth. For instance, former President James Wolfensohn justified the Bank's new foray into anticorruption matters by declaring that "corruption is . . . not political but it is social and it is economic and, therefore, I am allowed to talk about it. And if . . . politicians think that it is political, that is not my problem. I think it is social and economic. Therefore, I can talk about it" (2000). The Bank's embrace of such issues as good governance and anticorruption in the early 1990s could be attributed to such factors as the failure of structural adjustment programs, the end of the Cold War (which relaxed donor countries' concerns about the Bank encroaching on their sovereignty), and the rise of neoliberalism (which hailed the importance of institutions and dictated that the role of government is to secure the conditions for market integration). External pressure from civil society advocates and grassroots movements has also played an important role in the Bank's expansion of its agenda. Given the institution's recent embrace of more political issues, why has it still not adopted a human rights framework?

Before addressing this question, I will first describe the components that would form part of a potential human rights framework at the Bank. Given the varying meanings that employees attach to human rights, there is a plurality of possible agendas. One could classify them into a *consequentialist* approach (meaning the Bank would promote the realization of human rights) and a *deontological* approach (where the Bank would respect human rights, whether or not honoring this value promotes realization overall; Pettit 1989).

A human rights agenda under a consequentialist approach may entail creating a specialized department (like the Bank's current Social Development or Environment Departments) that would design projects directly targeting human rights and providing technical assistance for other projects to adopt a "rights-based approach to development." This typically requires institutional change and creation of accountability mechanisms so that human rights are treated as constitutive of the goal of development. As part of this approach, "agency mandates are redefined in human rights terms, seeking to create a more structural and holistic approach to development and social change. Here we face a fundamental rethinking of the entire development practice: its ideology, its partners, its aims, its processes, its systems and procedures" (Uvin 2004, 50). Country directors from the Bank may engage in policy dialogues over human rights with government representatives as part of their formulation of Country Assistance Strategies, which are written every two or three years. In addition, Bank staff may provide assistance to countries toward adapting their national laws according to international human rights standards.

A deontological approach may mean constraining loans on the basis of nonviolation of human rights by, for instance, applying a human rights impact assessment to all projects (which is similar to how environmental impact assessments are conducted for all projects). Such an assessment would likely be mandated by a human rights operational policy that would have to be approved by the Bank's Board of Executive Directors. A policy may include references to international human rights treaties as benchmarks, just as the Bank's environmental assessment policy cites international environmental conventions. In this way, a human rights agenda would be a systematic, institutionwide commitment to ensuring that Bank projects in all sectors do not directly or indirectly violate human rights. To build capacity among staff to carry out this type of human rights agenda, the Bank may have to institute training programs or hire specialized staff to carry out the assessments.

The Bank has fallen well short of adopting a human rights agenda under either definition. According to a book devoted to this issue, human rights have "(i) arisen only very selectively—and usually marginally—in a practical programmatic context; (ii) been of little practical relevance in the discharge of the Bank's social safeguard functions and assessment procedures; and (iii) been of at least marginal or 'inspirational' relevance to the Bank's research agenda and substantive policy development" (Darrow 2003, 25). My interviews have confirmed this observation. Given evidence of Bank projects that have indirectly or directly led to large-scale human rights violations (see Darrow 2003), the question remains as to why human rights have remained marginal for so many years.

To understand how agendas circulate and become embedded within a global institution like the Bank, we need to analyze two layers of politics: among member states as well as within the bureaucracy itself. My study looks beyond member state politics and focuses on the underemphasized bureaucratic obstacles arising from the Bank's organizational culture. I look inside the institution and analyze it as a set of discursive power relations that are inscribed in everyday practices.

The first layer of politics is within member states. The Bank is after all an instrument of global powers and reflects the struggles between the global North and South. The institution is influenced by the political interests of certain member countries, particularly the United States; this undermines its multilateral character and legitimacy abroad (Goldman 2005). Although member state politics was not the central subject of my research, the politics continuously operated in the background and shaped the perceptions and actions of the bureaucrats and activists I interviewed. As I explain in Chapter 2, the Bank's Board of Executive Directors is internally divided over the issue of human rights. Since the board operates by consensus, it will not approve a human rights agenda if there is opposition by member countries such as Saudi Arabia and China. Opposition by states is largely due to their fear that a human rights agenda would infringe on their sovereignty and may become a conditionality on lending for borrower countries, while not imposing similar restrictions on donor countries. They maintain that human rights is a "political" consideration that is restricted under the Bank's Articles of Agreement.

Although the Bank and the debate over human rights within it are structured by member state politics, there are openings for introducing human rights without board approval. The member states cast a shadow over the institution, but what has been underemphasized is the amount of decision-making autonomy held by employees and senior management in pushing issues forward under the board's radar. This is particularly true when member states hold competing preferences and do not reach consensus over issues. Employees then have discretion and the potential to significantly influence how the institution behaves. This was the case for the issue of anticorruption, which was eventually mainstreamed under the leadership of former President James Wolfensohn despite opposition from various member states. A critical factor in the mainstreaming process was the framing of anticorruption as an economic issue. The Bank presented its fight against corruption as "just another necessary technical instrument employed in the bundle of other technical measures, such as accounting and budgeting systems, to transform the state into an efficient machine that creates the enabling environment needed by private enterprise to boost economic growth" (Anders 2005, 52; internal quotations removed). Issues such as anticorruption and rule of law that were once controversial have been depoliticized in order to appeal to the dominant economic way of thinking.

Despite its neoliberal agenda of privatization, capital market liberalization, and deregulation, the Bank's interventions have the unintended "instrument-effects" of expanding the extent and reach of state power (Ferguson 1990). As a development institution, the Bank serves as an "'anti-politics machine,' depoliticizing everything it touches, everywhere whisking political realities out of sight, all the while performing, almost unnoticed, its own pre-eminently political operation of expanding bureaucratic state power" (1990, xv). It overcomes political challenges from outside "not only by enhancing the powers of administration and repression, but by insistently reposing political questions of land, resources, jobs, or wages as technical 'problems' responsive to the technical 'development' intervention" (270).

This effort to depoliticize issues using the metrics of economics is itself a political act and indicates why the Bank is in fact such a political institution. The process of commensuration (where information is reduced into numbers that can be compared) "changes the terms of what can be talked about, how we value, and how we treat what we value" (Espeland and Stevens 1998, 315). It rejects any notion of intrinsic value and fails to acknowledge that abstracting particular values into numbers may alter their meaning significantly. As we see clearly with regard to the Bank, commensuration is a means of managing uncertainty, depersonalizing relations, imposing control, securing legitimacy, and enforcing discipline (ibid.).

This brings us to the second layer of politics: politics within the bureaucracy, including a clash of expertise among staff. By studying the Bank as a bureaucracy, including its formal and informal norms, the incentive system, and decision-making processes, this book contributes to anthropological literature on development. I aim to expand upon James Ferguson's image of the development institution as an "anti-politics machine" (Ferguson 1990). Although he effectively examined the "instrument-effects" that stray from the institution's stated intentions for development projects, he did not address the internal operations within the institution that have led to this disjuncture. Both Ferguson and Arturo Escobar studied the discourse of development by looking at how institutional power is exercised in the daily social and economic life of communities and on how people think and act in local settings. What is missing is an ethnographic account of how development discourse produces "domains of objects and rituals of truth" in the daily life of the institution—i.e., the bureaucratic and textual mechanisms that structure the relations between client and agent (Foucault 1977, 194). Discourse is central to how institutions function. Borrowing from Foucault's notion of discourse as both an instrument and an effect of power, I concentrate on the latter in order to understand the former (Foucault 1978). My study focuses on human rights discourse and the politics of its circulation within the institution.

Competing Rationalities

The battle over human rights at the Bank has corresponded not only to a clash over the prevailing professional ethos within the organization, but also to a clash of normative rationalities: economics versus human rights, or more broadly, the market versus social democratic liberalism into which human rights nestles. Economic knowledge has become dominant within the world of bureaucracies as well as in domestic and international public

policy making. The Bank is both a producer and an effect of this phenomenon. It has facilitated the global expansion of capital through the mission
of poverty reduction but has also mirrored the effects of economic globalization in its bureaucratic practices, for instance through the quantification
of many issues that are value-laden and politically contested. This study
uncovers the tensions within the organization between forms of rationality as they are institutionalized. In particular, I analyze the clash between
experts over whether human rights is an incommensurable value that precludes trade-offs and should not be translated into an instrumental logic, or
whether economic rationality trumps all other concerns. By observing the
conditions under which these rationalities are contested within the Bank,
we can understand the competing values that underlie global governance
and how they are being negotiated.

In this study, I analyze the process by which economic rationality is
produced, circulated, and reproduced within the institution, and how it
intersects with the competing rationality of human rights. The encounter
between the knowledge regimes of economics and human rights has led to
two results: (1) infusing human rights discourse with an instrumental logic
and (2) uncovering the political dimensions of the economics and develop
ment discourses.

The story of human rights in the World Bank represents a broader depic-
tion of how these two knowledge regimes meet, clash, and intersect within
the context of an international institution. Interestingly, these regimes share
a common history in that the same neoliberal ideology that has fueled economic globalization has also mainstreamed the human rights discourse.
Both the international human rights system and the global economic regime
ultimately reinforce state power. Although human rights discourse has critiqued the unfulfilled promises of global governance institutions and served
as an instrument of resistance against state sovereignty, the international human rights system itself actually reifies state power. Despite being based on a
cosmopolitan foundation of common humanity without regard to national
origin or citizenship, human rights is embedded in an international legal
regime predicated on the cooperation of states. It is ultimately the state's
responsibility to guarantee human rights. Similarly, the global economic regime is centered around the Bretton Woods institutions (the World Bank
and the International Monetary Fund) and the World Trade Organization,

all of which are intergovernmental organizations that are largely governed by donor countries and conduct their operations by way of states.

They both claim universality and share a commitment to individual autonomy, but the knowledge regimes of economics and human rights operate through distinctive logics. Mainstream economics is a discipline based on the value of efficiency, perfect markets, rational actors, and resource constraints. It is presented as a positive science founded on a consequentialist rationale that is concerned with outcomes. Its goals include the maximization of an individual's utility, including her monetary income and social welfare. Human rights theory, by contrast, adopts a deontological approach, concerned with principles that are important regardless of their consequences. It is premised on the inherent dignity of persons and a system of universal, inalienable truths from which are derived absolute freedoms and basic duties. Human rights theory consists of an ethical dimension, which is predicated on moral norms based on natural or prelegal rights, and a legal dimension where rights are prescribed by law.

Putting aside these distinctive logics, we can posit that both economics and human rights are normative theories (in that they offer judgments as to which policies are best for society) that *can* be wielded in an instrumental fashion (whether or not they do so in practice). In theory, there is a human rights dimension to economics and an economic dimension to human rights; "asserting human rights demands economic means, . . . and efficacy and efficiency of the agent's economic decisions presupposes a significant degree of liberty" (Branco 2009, 8). Even though the two discourses share a common objective of promoting human welfare, they rarely intersect in practice. Economics and human rights have trouble communicating, with the former speaking the language of wants and the latter the language of rights. Under economics, goods and services can be unequally distributed, which does not comply with a human rights approach. Most economists struggle to accommodate human rights within an orthodox econometric calculus: "As 'externalities' economists are prone to rendering them, at best, as peculiarities that often challenge rational (that is to say, welfare-maximising) economic analysis, or at worst as efficiency-distorting irrelevancies" (Kinley 2006, 367–68). They treat human rights as a competing rather than a complementing discourse. Given the divergence between the two discourses and those who subscribe to them, the question then becomes whether and how human rights can become institutionalized in an organization like the Bank where the prevailing ethos is economic rationality.

Yet this is a story of more than just human rights. It is more generally about the entrance of normative discourses with universal claims into the Bank, and how they are transformed in the process. This transformation uncovers contradictions within the discourse of development and the spurious distinction between economics and politics. The struggle to bring human rights into the Bank yields a valuable observation. Though Bank officials have continuously tried to present the institution as apolitical, their attempt to avoid the political sphere by appealing to economics is futile.

Economics, the reigning discipline behind development, is a normative worldview fraught with assumptions and political motivations. Underlying economic ideology is an abstract representation of the Economy that can be replicated around the world regardless of national context and historical variations. The universalistic rhetoric of economics has facilitated its diffusion across countries regardless of local context. But economics "is always and everywhere a political endeavor" in that its choices for the appropriate structures for society have political implications (Fourcade 2009, 125). Some scholars have even argued that cost-benefit analysis is simply "an ex post justification for decisions that have long since been made on political grounds" (Payer 1982, 80).

To avoid political underpinnings, economics relies on numbers to achieve objectivity. It features a formalist language that is supposedly produced under a process of rationalization, thus granting a "symbolic effectiveness" that creates "an effect of consecration and permission" (Bourdieu 1987; 1990, 85). It presumes a scientific authority through a rhetoric of quantification and a technical language of truth, using such expressions as "it is obvious that," "it is evident," "doubtless," "easily seen," and "we may expect" (McCloskey 1985, 17). Quantification acts as a "technology of distance" by appealing to objectivity and universality without reliance on local knowledge (Porter 1995, ix). Objectivity through numbers thus becomes a proxy for truth and fairness. In her study of human rights indicators, Sally Engle Merry contends that

> numbers convey an aura of objective truth and facilitate comparisons.
> [They] conceal their political and theoretical origins and underlying theories

of social change and activism. . . . A key dimension of the power of indicators [and other technologies of audit] is their capacity to convert complicated, contextually variable phenomena into unambiguous, clear, and impersonal measures. They represent a technology of producing readily accessible and standardized forms of knowledge [2011, 5].

As I demonstrate in this study, human rights are being accommodated within the economic calculus of the Bank as a normative technology of audit (see Strathern 2000).

By conflating "development" with *economic* development, the Bank has strived to confer upon the enterprise the same objective, rational properties seemingly held by economics. A guise of scientific authority masks the fallacies of development enterprises—e.g., that it promotes internal equality and enables poor countries to "catch up" with "developed" ones (Parajuli 1991, 181). In fact, development discourse is "generated by very different and diverse administrative, political [and] socio-relational logics which are concealed by rationalizing policy" (Mosse 2005, 22). It serves as a form of imperialism in representation and a mechanism of truth production that reflects institutionalized power relations (Escobar 1995). As the ideology of development has become naturalized and uncontested, it has become hegemonic. Its power operates below the surface and beyond the consciousness of actors (Comaroff and Comaroff 1991). These actors include not only the subjects of development but also many of the so-called development experts who are designing and implementing development projects and policies.

I argue that we need to look inside the bureaucracy in order to understand competing forms of knowledge that inform development institutions such as the Bank. My analysis of Bank bureaucrats borrows from recent work on expertise, including the socialization practices through which a bureaucratic self is made (Brenneis 1994). Influenced by Michel Foucault, it examines how expertise reproduces power relations by asserting who controls valued knowledge. Using human rights as a lens through which to analyze the politics of expertise within the institution, I contend that the interpretive frameworks of Bank lawyers and economists correspond to Weber's distinction between instrumental rationality and value rationality (two forms of subjective rational action; see Espeland 1998; Weber 1978). Even though many lawyers conceive of human rights as legal imperatives, having an intrinsic value and derived from the international human rights regime, most economists emphasize its instrumental value, as a means towards achieving other objectives such as economic development. The interaction between these competing frameworks raises the important question of whether human rights can be translated and if so, at what cost.

The Translation of Human Rights

My work extends the anthropological study of human rights as a social practice (see, e.g., Goodale and Merry 2007) and analyzes its translation within a bureaucracy of experts. In this study, I demonstrate how the convergence of human rights with economic globalization imbues rights with a technocratic rationality through a process of delegalization and depoliticization. This process uncovers the multiple logics that encompass human rights, including the regulatory and sovereignty dimensions. The sovereignty dimension invokes the universal character, symbolic valence, and emancipatory power of human rights, while the regulatory dimension emphasizes the instrumental, rule-oriented, and administrative qualities that are more susceptible to a market logic.

I argue that the regulatory and sovereignty dimensions are critical to the concept of human rights. They are necessarily linked even though their intersection is fraught with tensions and contradictions. Goals of justice and fairness can conflict with those of economic efficiency. Yet if the political potential of human rights is negated, the rights lose their teeth and are rendered not just impotent but transformed into a form one can no longer call "human rights."

In light of prohibitions against political activities in its Articles of Agreement, the Bank has embraced what it interprets as the economic-related aspects of rights, which make up their regulatory dimension, and is attempting to vacate their sovereignty dimension. For instance, although the Bank has adopted a policy on indigenous rights (largely as a result of external pressure), it has largely limited the focus to economic-related issues such as land rights and the commercial development of cultural resources. It has refused to engage in sovereignty-related aspects such as indigenous rights to self-determination. Yet my account reveals that a lively debate has continued to thrive within the institution over which human rights are actionable.

In exploring the regulatory dimension of human rights as revealed in a bureaucratic setting, my project examines the process of norm translation in a new context. Most anthropologists address the adoption and translation of norms by social movements, NGOs, and local communities; I focus instead on the actors that govern, work within, and lobby an international institution. Taking into account the knowledge practices and power dynamics among these actors, I found that the "vernacularization" process in the Bank (whereby norms are adapted to local meanings) is a continuous struggle among actors over whether and how much to translate human rights (see Merry 2006b). For example, even though some lawyers and NGO activists feared that translating human rights into an economic framework would dilute the substance, others recognized the practical demand to appeal to economists and adapt the human rights framework accordingly.

The conversion of human rights into an instrumental framework has been called "human rights mainstreaming" (Koskenniemi 2010), which is a bureaucratized logic adopted by institutions like the Bank as they transform human rights into a depoliticized technology. But this act of depoliticization is profoundly political since it conceals the ideological practices behind the development industry—including the expansion of bureaucratic power, the reproduction of hierarchies of society (the "developed" world over the "developing"), and the objectification of the poor. The translation of human rights into a technical discourse emasculates what would be an emancipatory framework and strips the subjects of development of their capacity to make universal claims for justice. In other words, depoliticizing human rights subordinates them to the imperative of economic growth and "extends that subordination through the formation of the developmental subject, a subject whose very humanity is now delimited according to the demands of market logic" (Pahuja 2007, 70).

The political struggle over translating human rights at the Bank is part of a larger debate occurring in a variety of settings. For instance, in the "war" against terrorism, there is a lively discussion over how to balance the right to freedom from torture against risks to national security. Those who view human rights as trumps argue that "there must be some limit to the weighing of costs and benefits—that some requirements are so self-evidently 'good' (or some forms of behavior so intrinsically 'evil') that they should leave no room to instrumental calculations" (Koskenniemi 2010, 48). In other words, human rights should serve as trump cards that override concerns about economic efficiency (2010) and should not be subject to trade-offs (see Dworkin 1977; Sarat and Kearns 2001). In contrast to this position, those who support a human rights mainstreaming approach argue that human rights is one policy among others and so administrators should balance their concern for human rights along with other policies when making decisions. Yet this approach also brings with it additional challenges, such as how one compares qualitative concerns with quantitative ones, and whether certain rights should be prioritized just because they are easier to articulate in an instrumental language.

The translation of human rights raises a number of additional questions and dilemmas. Is there a point where human rights norms are translated so far that they lose their essential core, particularly the sovereignty dimension that is critical to the concept? A related issue is the difficulty of determining whether actors consider a translation meaningful or simply strategic, "where local political actors overlay other distinctive political projects with the legitimating mantle of rights, but to which they may have only a fleeting and expedient commitment" (Wilson 2007, 359). Such a determination could suggest whether the invocation of human rights is mere window dressing or part of a larger neoliberal project of social justice.

Methods

My ethnography of the Bank traces the role of human rights within the organization by studying its everyday workings.[4] I examine the Bank from the top down as well as the bottom up, focusing not only on leadership and administrative structure but also on the tasks and incentives of employees. I attempt to uncover the underlying organizational culture and the contradictions and tensions within it, including competing subcultures that divide along disciplinary and geographic lines, among others. Internal contestations array economists against lawyers, for example, and lower-level staff in operations units against managers in advisory units. My anthropological analysis of the Bank's organizational culture allowed me to in a sense "live with" the employees I studied by engaging in direct, firsthand observation of their daily behavior at work and participating in their activities. By doing so, I was able to uncover the internal dynamics that shape how human rights norms are framed and implemented. I also studied the informal practices and unspoken assumptions held by employees that may be misinterpreted by or hidden from external observers, as well as from the employees themselves.

Prior studies of the Bank have failed to account for the internal divisions between departments and individuals, instead treating it as a monolithic institution (see, e.g., Danaher 1994; Payer 1982; Price 1989; Shihata 1991b, 1995, 2000a). More recent studies undertaken by sociologists, economists, and political scientists have focused on the Bank as a network of social relations, an apparatus of financial hegemony and global capital, or a neoliberal policy-making institution. Yet such studies do not account for the internal pressures felt by some Bank employees, for instance, who are torn between hopes for internal reform of social policies and the need to comply with operational procedures. Particular forms of social consciousness are embedded within the Bank that only participant observation can uncover.

This study is based on ethnographic fieldwork that I conducted at the Bank headquarters in Washington, D.C., for a total of approximately two years over the period 2002–2006. During the summers of 2002 and 2004, I engaged in preliminary fieldwork as a consultant and intern in the Social Development and Environment Departments for Latin America and the Caribbean Region, and in the Legal Department. During 2002, I observed how employees implement and apply, or choose not to apply, the Bank's indigenous peoples policy in development projects. This experience uncovered the complications that often arise in the Bank when social goals compete with economic incentives within the institution. My work at the Bank during 2004 included researching an Inspection Panel case on resettlement resulting from a dam project in Argentina[5] and writing a report on land conflict and indigenous peoples in Colombia. While interning in the Legal Department, I became familiar with the Bank's safeguard policies as I established relationships with employees in the Environmental and International Law Unit. These employees later introduced me to a variety of their colleagues in the Legal Department when I returned in September 2005 to conduct full-time fieldwork.

During 2003–04, I had the opportunity to consult with the Bank as a designated "human rights focal point" for the Europe and Central Asia (ECA) region. The human rights focal points were created in late 2003 to assess each geographic region's contribution to and impact on human rights. I was hired for this position by a lawyer in the ECA region whom I had met during the summer of 2002. After conducting archival research and semistructured interviews, I coauthored a report with her on the Bank's contribution to human rights in Europe and Central Asia. The report was part of a Bank-wide stock-taking exercise of the institution's activities and evolving position on human rights. After writing the report, I witnessed the politics around its circulation within the institution, which gave me firsthand experience with the difficulties of internalizing human rights at the Bank.

My position as a consultant and intern for two summers afforded me the trust to obtain access as a researcher for a full year of fieldwork, from September 2005 until July 2006. During this time, I also served as a part-time consultant with the Agriculture and Rural Development Unit for Latin America and the Caribbean Region, for which I wrote a report on indigenous peoples and land reform projects in the region. My employment was necessary for me to gain entrée to the institution (including a World Bank email account and ID card, and access to the intranet site). Moreover, serving as a consultant gave me legitimacy when I requested interviews from employees, even though I was always careful to note that I was concurrently conducting research on the institution.

My fieldwork during 2005–06 included interviews with more than seventy former and current employees (from project managers to a former president), executive directors on the Bank's board, U.S. Treasury officials, and NGO representatives; analysis of Bank projects and reports; observations at Bank training sessions and seminars; and observations at NGO meetings and conferences. I restricted my research to the Bank's Washington, D.C., headquarters, as opposed to field offices, and had the most contact with the employees in the three departments where I worked (although I tried to interview a cross-section of employees across departments and ranking). My primary method of obtaining interviews with high-level officials was through referrals from my previous interviewees. When I observed meetings or interviewed employees, I described the purpose of my research and obtained their informed consent. Almost all interviews were recorded and transcribed, and they were conducted under the condition that I not use the employees' names. Unless I was given consent to disclose their identity, I list only their current (or former) position and department.

My contacts with various civil society organizations stemmed from my summer 2001 internship at the Indian Law Resource Center in Washington,

D.C., a small indigenous-rights NGO that served as a key participant in the consultation process over the revision of the Bank's indigenous peoples policy. As an intern, I had had the opportunity to observe consultation meetings with the Bank and to participate in strategy sessions with fellow human rights NGOs, including the Bank Information Center, Forest Peoples Program, Center for International Environmental Law, and Amazon Alliance, organizations that I later contacted when conducting my fieldwork.

In the context of my ethnography of the Bank, being a participant observer meant taking on at least three roles and concurrently serving as both an insider and an outsider. One role was that of an external researcher, analyzing the institution from an outsider's point of view. A second role was as intern and consultant, participating firsthand in the work of the institution and interacting with other employees in the context of their day-to-day work. Finally, I briefly took on the role of an advocate, while serving as a human rights focal point for the ECA region in 2004. My background in human rights legal advocacy and my previous work on indigenous rights gave me a preconception that the Bank should become more involved in promoting and protecting human rights. This attitude colored my framing of questions to interviewees and the analysis of my data, thus confirming that there is a "slippage between the role of activist and scholar and [an] impossibility of separating them" (Merry 2005, 243). After all, "academic and activist endeavors are never autonomous, despite our analytical assumptions of separateness" (243). My personal engagement with the subject of my research clearly shaped my study in various ways, but it also gave me access I might not have had otherwise.

Structure of the Book

In Chapter 1, I explain why the Bank's approach to human rights (or lack thereof) appears counterintuitive. I first elaborate on the external pressure on the Bank to adopt a human rights agenda. Compared to other international institutions and aid agencies, the Bank stands as an outlier in terms of its approach to human rights. In addition, commercial banks and the Bank's own private sector arm—the International Finance Corporation—have more openly embraced human rights out of concern for their public image and reputation. Their activities, as well as lobbying by the United Nations and NGOs, have pressured the Bank to more explicitly incorporate human rights into its work. Yet NGO efforts have been stymied by the lack of consensus among advocates and their unwillingness to reach out to Bank staff to forge an internal-external alliance. In the second part of Chapter 1, I describe internal campaigns since the early 1990s to pressure Bank management to adopt a human rights agenda. I argue that past attempts have failed for a number of reasons, including a clash of expertise, turf wars between departments, insufficient resources, and a failure to mobilize external support to bolster internal campaigns.

In the remainder of the book, I tell the story of *why* human rights has remained marginal despite the internal and external pressure that would suggest otherwise. In Chapter 2, I describe the political and legal obstacles that scholars and advocates commonly cite as reasons for the marginality of human rights at the Bank. The political obstacles stem from opposition by some member countries on the Bank's Board of Executive Directors, while the legal obstacles arise from the its Articles of Agreement. My research suggests that these obstacles are not as significant as one would expect and that internal factors are playing an underemphasized but nonetheless important role.

The end of Chapter 2 describes the implications of an important event in 2006: the issuing of the Legal Opinion on Human Rights by the departing general counsel. The opinion addressed the central legal obstacle—particular restrictions in the Articles of Agreement—that had long served as a primary reason the Bank could not directly engage in human rights. It also gave the Legal Department, which had played a minimal role in earlier initiatives within the Bank, an opportunity to shape discussion of a possible human rights strategy. After conducting a textual analysis of the opinion, I contend that its failure to generate organizational change was due to ambiguity over its legal status and resulting uncertainty about whether the Legal Department should circulate it as the Bank's "official" interpretation of the Articles. Another reason, which I discuss in Chapter 3, is internal conflict within the department over value-laden issues such as human rights.

Chapter 3 analyzes the practices and status of Bank lawyers within the larger bureaucracy as well as the aforementioned clash of expertise among staff. I first analyze the Bank's organizational culture, including internal decision-making process and formal and informal processes of norm socialization. I also examine the incentives and operational policies that influence what employees value and how they reconcile competing goals. I then describe the production and circulation of knowledge within the organization and how that relates to the Bank's management structure. Finally, I analyze power dynamics between professional subcultures, whose members speak distinct languages and exhibit particular norms arising from their disciplinary training. I focus on the prestige of economists and the lower status of lawyers in the Legal Department, which exhibits internal conflict and a culture of secrecy. I argue that the clash of expertise in the Bank has served as a critical bureaucratic obstacle in achieving human rights norm internalization.

Chapter 4 demonstrates how the clash of expertise among staff has played out over the issue of human rights. I first analyze the evolution of human rights as a taboo in the institution and describe how the type and extent of the taboo has changed over time and in different contexts. I then examine interpretive battles between Bank employees subscribing to an intrinsic framework for valuing human rights and those who adopt an instrumental framework. To demonstrate the operational implications of these competing interpretive frameworks, I compare two projects, in Russia and St. Lucia, that applied divergent approaches to the rights of people living with HIV/AIDS. I suggest that reconciliation between the frameworks requires "translators" who move between disciplinary communities and can bridge interpretive gaps (Merry 2006b).

Finally, I discuss the most recent attempt to introduce human rights into the Bank, led by members of the Legal Department. After repeated failures to mobilize staff behind an intrinsic framework for human rights, Bank lawyers have conceded to the dominant economic ethos within the institution. They have recently pursued an incremental strategy of framing human rights for economists, or what I call economizing human rights. I argue that this strategy has met with early success because its leaders are learning from the failures of prior attempts as they adapt their approach to the Bank's organizational culture. Yet internal struggles persist in the Legal Department and among the lawyers themselves over whether to define human rights in an economic framework. These internal struggles reveal a tension between principles and pragmatism—i.e., between pursuing normative, intangible values and goals, and finding a practical approach for solving problems (which may make it necessary to reconcile competing principles).

The concluding chapter analyzes the implications of economizing human rights in light of a growing trend among corporations to adopt a risk-management approach to the issue. I also review the history of the anticorruption agenda at the Bank and highlight possible similarities to the mainstreaming of human rights. Finally, I suggest areas for future research and highlight contributions of this study to scholarship in anthropology, international law, and international relations.

Chapter 1

Behind the Curve

Institutional Resistance to Human Rights

WHY IS IT SURPRISING that human rights has been such a marginal issue at the World Bank? If the institution is a bank, after all, why should we expect it to incorporate human rights norms into its activities? There are a number of reasons the Bank's approach to human rights (or lack thereof) appears counterintuitive.

Over the past two decades, the Bank has been a leader in promoting particular development issues that it has interpreted as central to a mandate of poverty reduction. These issues include environmental sustainability, which the Bank began to interpret as a core objective during the 1980s after decades of grassroots activism, growing evidence of the environmental costs of Bank-sponsored projects, and its own need to develop alternative rationales for an interventionist development mission (Rajagopal 2003, 113–27; see also Wade 1997). Although the Bank has taken pride in serving as a norm setter among development agencies on the environment, why hasn't it taken the initiative to serve as a leader on standards relating to human rights?

Compared to other international institutions and aid agencies, the Bank stands as an outlier in terms of its approach to human rights. For instance, the United Nations Development Programme has begun to implement a rights-based approach (UNDP 2005), while the Bank's implicit human rights work has been criticized by development experts as rhetorical and ad hoc (Uvin 2004). The Bank's approach also stands in contrast to that of many private financial institutions. Because of a concern for their public image and the reputational and legal risks of committing human rights abuses, some corporations are beginning to take steps toward becoming more socially responsible by adopting such tools as human rights impact assessments. In fact, the International Finance Corporation (IFC), the Bank's private-sector arm, has openly adopted a human rights agenda as part of a risk management approach, under a market-based operational logic. This approach translates international human rights norms for the business community by defining potential human rights violations as strategic risks, which may damage a company's reputation, threaten its profits, and lead to possible litigation.[1] However, the IFC's selective engagement in human rights has been subject to criticism by nongovernmental organizations (NGOs).[2]

Moreover, civil society organizations and internal advocates have pressed the Bank to integrate human rights considerations into projects and programs. One would expect the Bank to have been swayed by this pressure, as well as by the growing trend of corporations and development agencies to address human rights more openly. Yet it has not been so swayed. In this chapter, I elaborate on the external and internal pressure on the Bank over the past two decades to adopt a human rights agenda.

External Pressure

International Organizations and Aid Agencies

Over the past two decades, international organizations and aid agencies have increasingly recognized an interdependence between human rights and development. There are several reasons for this change of thinking: (1) the end of the Cold War, which brought a sense of missionary zeal; (2) the failure of structural adjustment programs and a greater emphasis on good governance and democracy; and (3) the redefinition of development as more than economic growth (Uvin 2007, 597). As evidence of this growing consensus, the 1993 Vienna World Conference Declaration affirmed, "Democracy, development and respect for human rights and fundamental freedoms are interdependent and mutually reinforcing. . . . The international community should support the strengthening and promoting of democracy, development and respect for human rights and fundamental freedoms in the entire world" (para. 8). The United Nations' 2000 Millennium Summit and its 2005 World Summit reiterated this declaration and spurred the adoption of new policy frameworks among bilateral and multilateral agencies.

The United Nations has been leading the way in incorporating human rights concerns into development policies. In 1990, it began promoting a human development approach, which offers an alternative view of development to the neoliberal paradigm of the Washington Consensus. This approach defines development as not only generating economic growth but also distributing its benefits equitably, and it promotes a conception of well-being that goes beyond the economic. It is applied in the UN's Human Development Reports, published annually by the UNDP since 1990 (see Fukuda-Parr 2003). The UN has since begun mainstreaming human rights in all of its activities, as announced in the 1997 report "Renewing the United Nations: A Programme for Reform." As part of this effort, the UNDP (which is not hampered by the political prohibitions that exist in the Bank's Articles of Agreement) adopted a rights-based approach to development (UNDP 2005).

Many bilateral and multilateral aid agencies have followed the UN's lead and adopted human rights policies or a rights-based approach to development. A recent study conducted by the Organization for Economic Cooperation and Development (OECD) compares the Bank's approach to those of other donor agencies. It found that the Bank stands on one end of a continuum, which classifies methods of integrating human rights into development strategies (Piron and O'Neil 2006). The methods range from a rights-based approach and human rights mainstreaming to human rights dialogue and human rights projects, and finally to implicit human rights work (2006). Most agencies (including the European Commission, UNICEF, and many bilateral agencies) fall within the three middle categories—human rights mainstreaming, dialogue, and projects—while the Bank falls within the last category of implicit human rights work. When a working draft of the OECD study was presented to Bank staff in April 2006, the deputy general counsel acknowledged that "rhetorical repackaging" describes how the Bank has traditionally approached human rights, although the Bank is striving to move further on the continuum.

Given the Bank's position as an outlier among international institutions and aid agencies in terms of its approach to human rights, representatives from the UN, the academic community, and the OECD have pressured the Bank to more explicitly address human rights. In March 2004, the former UN High Commissioner for Human Rights, Mary Robinson, and a New York University law professor, Philip Alston, convened a conference at New York University School of Law on "Human Rights and Development: Towards Mutual Reinforcement" (see Alston and Robinson 2005). The purpose of the conference, which also featured legal scholars and senior vice presidents from the Bank, was for the Bank to share its existing human-rights-related activities and learn more about the UN's practice on human rights and development. Similar meetings have occurred over the past few years between members of the Bank's Legal Department and UN representatives in Geneva. These interactions have pressured the Bank to reflect on its approach to human rights, although they did not directly lead to substantive changes in Bank policy.

The International Finance Corporation and the Private Sector

Another source of external pressure on the Bank has been the International Finance Corporation, which lends money to corporations in emerging markets. Since 2002, the IFC has become a stronger promoter of human rights than the Bank by promoting such initiatives as a human rights impact assessment to corporate clients. The IFC's support for human rights is due to pressure from corporations, which are concerned with their public image and are subject to competitive pressures. Given that the IFC is moving beyond the Bank in explicitly incorporating human rights concerns into its operations, NGOs have recently lobbied the Bank to adopt a human rights approach that is at least as progressive as that of its private sector arm. Moreover, the private sector has increasingly been competing with the Bank to fund projects in such emerging markets as China and India. This competition has pressured the Bank to conform to private industry standards on social responsibility.

Since 2002, when then Executive Vice President Peter Woicke publicly announced the institution's commitment to human rights, the IFC has been facilitating the translation of human rights norms for the private sector. It is leveraging a leadership role among financial institutions to set standards on how to operationalize human rights. In a discussion note on the topic, the IFC explained its role in promoting the UN Global Compact, a set of nine corporate social responsibility principles on human rights, labor, and environmental issues:[3]

> As a development institution, IFC does not see itself in competition with commercial banks, rather it aims to advance the debate on difficult issues, through

providing technical assistance if necessary, and convince others to follow by demonstrating what can work in practice. IFC is seeking to make the race to the top (as opposed to a race to the bottom) real. In this way, IFC can help translate the debate at the Global Compact into the emerging markets context, and help increase the volume of responsible investments in those markets.[4]

One of the IFC's first steps in promoting corporate social responsibility was to take on the role of chief broker for the Equator Principles, standards for private sector banks that are modeled on the IFC's social and environmental policies.

The Equator Principles were originally conceived in October 2002 when the IFC invited a group of major private banks to discuss an environmental and social risk-assessment framework for the projects they finance that are over $50 million in size. These projects often include oil and gas pipelines and hydroelectric dams, which are particularly prone to causing environmental and social disruption. The preamble states, "We will not provide loans to projects where the borrower will not or is unable to comply with our respective social and environmental policies and procedures that implement the Equator Principles."[5] The principles are to be incorporated into loan covenants, thereby holding borrower countries accountable for any failure to comply. Although activists have argued that the standards do not go far enough and lack a monitoring and enforcement mechanism, the Equator Principles are representative of a shift toward greater human rights accountability on the part of private banks.

The IFC's involvement with the Equator Principles prompted engagement with human rights when it adopted new operational policies. In 2003, the IFC began to revise its policies, which had been modeled on those of the World Bank's, and issued new "performance standards" in 2006. As part of this process, the institution received internal support to more forthrightly address human rights issues and what they mean for private sector clients. Although the IFC did not adopt a freestanding performance standard on human rights, it strengthened provisions in the areas of labor and working conditions and projects' use of private or public security personnel. In 2007, the IFC released a draft Guide to Human Rights Impact Assessment and Management, in collaboration with the International Business Leaders Forum and the UN Global Compact. The guide is intended as a tool for the private sector to address human rights concerns and is currently being piloted to evaluate potential human rights impacts in a number of IFC projects.

NGOs have questioned why the World Bank has not similarly developed a human rights impact assessment for its own projects. Given that the IFC and World Bank are sister institutions with the same Board of Executive Directors, it appears inconsistent that one institution would directly engage in human rights while the other would claim that the issue is too political. The primary reason for their disparate policies is that the two institutions have different clients; the World Bank lends to country governments while the IFC lends to corporations that then carry out projects in poor countries. According to a Human Rights Watch representative, "the IFC is more progressive-minded, but it's also less constrained because it's dealing with the private sector. So there are natural limits on what it's going to address anyway. And that allows them to be more focused, [and] to deal with issues that are less controversial in the business world . . . like human rights and security . . . and core labor rights."[6] Many corporations are expressing at least minimal commitment to human rights and environmental sustainability, which they view as instrumental in maintaining their reputation, hedging risks, and differentiating themselves from competitors.

Given their enormous international financial leverage, corporations have been finding themselves under intense scrutiny for direct or indirect involvement in reprehensible activities within the borders of host countries, particularly human rights abuses. Corporations can be complicit in human rights abuses in several ways: ignoring violations in situations of violent conflict, exacerbating such situations, generating revenues that governments use to commit violations, and engaging in corruption and bribery with state officials. And they can be involved in more direct violations of human rights, as in seizing an indigenous people's territory and thus violating their rights to land, culture, and livelihood. There have been a variety of efforts to hold businesses liable for human rights violations and responsible for the promotion of human rights. These efforts include regulations, marketplace incentives, and litigation in U.S. courts through the Alien Tort Claims Act.[7] The most recent initiatives to create regulatory structures have been the UN Global Compact and the UN Draft Norms on the Responsibilities of Transnational Corporations and Other Business Enterprises with Regard to Human Rights (see Ratner 2001; Weissbrodt and Kruger 2003).[8] Yet the Global Compact and the UN Draft Norms are not binding and have failed to close the gap between theory and practice. There have been recent developments that may address this gap. In 2011, the UN Human Rights Council endorsed the Guiding Principles on Business and Human Rights developed by John Ruggie, former Special Representative to the UN Secretary-General.[9]

To deflect the threat of governmental regulation and international initiatives to develop binding legal mechanisms, corporations tilted the meaning of corporate social responsibility (CSR) toward business interests as they campaigned for voluntary, non-enforceable guidelines and codes of conduct (Shamir 2004, 3, 7). Many have questioned whether these forms of self-regulation actually have an impact on corporate behavior, or whether they simply serve as window dressing and facilitate "greenwashing" by rewarding empty commitments and reporting for its own sake. By shaping the scope and contours of this field as one of self-regulation, corporations are deradicalizing the CSR field as they "disseminat[e] the neo-liberal logic of altruistic social participation that is to be governed by good will alone" (9). Their transformation of CSR into a risk management tool commodifies critique and incorporates it into a business opportunity. By legitimizing "an economization of authority" and constructing "a depoliticized framework of market-embedded discourse" (Shamir 2010, 14), CSR initiatives are part of the neoliberal practice of grounding sociomoral concerns within the instrumental rationality of markets.

Feeling pressure from civil society through consumer boycotts and popular protests, corporations have requested guidance from the IFC to advise them on social and environmental issues. As a result, as one IFC employee remarked, the situation has changed from the time "when internal and external people looked upon the environment and social [policies] from IFC as an add-on or an additional cost of doing business, to a point where in two years, it went . . . to 85% of the project finance market being governed by the same environmental and social guidelines and policies as our own" (referring to the widespread adoption of the Equator Principles modeled on IFC policies).[10] As the IFC and the private sector appear to move ahead of the Bank with regard to their approach to human rights, the Bank is facing demands to raise its standards and serve as the norm setter among international institutions. Yet as I elaborate below, external pressure has been surprisingly weaker than one would have expected, which is due to internal disagreement and lack of coordination among NGOs as well as their failure to form alliances with internal advocates.

Nongovernmental Organizations

NGOs have historically played an important role in pushing the Bank to adopt reforms, particularly on environmental and social issues. Countless groups, such as Fifty Years Is Enough and the Bretton Woods Project, protest at the Bank and IMF annual meetings and at project sites, where they often collaborate with local grassroots protest movements. Some NGOs have advocated for complete elimination of the Bretton Woods institutions; others have been instrumental in bringing about more public accountability to civil societies in both donor and borrower countries (Fox and Brown 1998). Their efforts resulted in creation of the Inspection Panel in 1993, a quasi-independent forum for local citizens to file complaints against the Bank for failure to follow its own policies (see Bradlow 1994), as well as the Bank's adoption of operational policies on involuntary resettlement, environmental assessment, and indigenous peoples. Since the early 1990s, NGOs within the Northern industrial countries and across the developing South have formed transnational coalitions as they campaigned for reform.

For instance, Ecuadorian environmental and indigenous organizations engaged with Northern environmental NGOs in their "Amazon for Life" campaign, which began in 1990 and demanded accountability and monitoring of extractive activities in the Amazon region (Treakle 1998, 225–26). The North/South NGO network was critical in targeting the pollution, deforestation, and cultural destruction by multinational oil companies and multilateral development banks (including a proposed World Bank loan for increased oil exploration) and organizing international boycotts of such companies as Texaco. Local and national advocacy organizations benefited in a variety of ways from the transnational alliances. Northern NGOs had better access to companies headquartered in those regions, they could lobby World Bank executive directors and appropriate government agencies on behalf of local NGOs, and they had the financial resources to support international activities. The Amazon for Life campaign has grown to include hundreds of environmental and human rights organizations (ibid.).

Despite the history of well-organized campaigns on behalf of the environment and indigenous peoples, NGOs have not successfully united on a campaign for the adoption of a human rights agenda at the Bank (although there have been isolated examples of advocacy). For instance, the executive director of Human Rights Watch met several times with then Bank Presidents James Wolfensohn and Paul Wolfowitz, but the organization has not organized any substantive follow-up. Another prominent human rights organization, Amnesty International, has been less involved. Although it has taken on a rights-based approach to development as an overarching priority, much of its work is targeted around distantly related issues such as the human rights implications of foreign investment contracts. The most active advocacy groups have been the Bank Information Center (BIC) and indigenous rights NGOs, although their work is largely case specific, project-oriented, and targeted at the rights of specific affected communities.

One would have expected that BIC in particular to have already developed a clear agenda on this issue, given that it has long served as a leader in pushing for reforms among multilateral development banks. Yet at the time I interviewed the policy director, he admitted that the organization had not yet formulated a position on how the Bank should operationalize a human rights approach:

> We don't have a set policy or position paper for BIC about the Bank and human rights. But kind of through consensus, our position is that the banks— all the development banks—have human rights obligations. Their operations impact the human rights of people. They need to be more clear about how their operations can impact the pursuit of rights of affected people. And in egregious cases, we feel that there should be greater accountability of the institutions. And we see that as a huge gap in the international system—that the banks cannot be brought forward to anyone in some sort of argument about complicity or facilitation of some sort of egregious human rights violation. What that would mean in practice, we're still not sure. . . . We don't have much of a strategy now. We haven't figured out where to go and what to do now.[11]

What explains the absence of an NGO strategy to actively lobby the Bank on human rights?

I discovered some of the challenges to a united NGO campaign when I was invited to attend a closed two-day workshop among NGOs in February 2006. The organizers of the workshop had hoped to generate consensus over possible advocacy strategies for holding development banks up to international human rights standards. However, there existed a significant divide among the NGOs over how to operationalize human rights at the Bank. Some focused on possible legal and judicial avenues to hold the Bank responsible for violations of international human rights law, or on the creation of an external accountability mechanism for multilateral development banks. Others wanted to lobby what was then the UN Sub-Commission on the Promotion and Protection of Human Rights (currently called the Human Rights Council Advisory Committee) to draft new guidelines on the obligations of international financial institutions. Finally, several NGO representatives favored less radical reforms focused within the Bank, such as greater internal compliance with existing operational policies or the adoption of a human rights assessment tool for projects like one used by the IFC. These varied strategies reflect the different priorities and competencies of NGOs, some of which are more policy-oriented and have experience lobbying the UN, while others prefer case-based legal strategies.

Advocates claimed that they found it challenging to come up with a strategy for implementing human rights in the Bank because they are not familiar enough with its internal operations and disagree on the most effective tactics for bringing about change. A Human Rights Watch representative observed:

> I think that because human rights groups, ourselves included, have not been very good at articulating an operationalized message about what it means to implement [human] rights, we still have this kind of dissonance between some Bank staff and ourselves when we talk about it. And part of it is our own lack of knowledge in some cases. . . . And I think there's still a learning curve, not only on the Bank's part but on our part too. If you look at the wide range of Bank activities, I don't think we have a comprehensive analysis to know precisely all the different ways where there can be a human rights impact.[12]

This purported lack of knowledge on the part of NGOs such as Human Rights Watch suggests the limited resources they have devoted to familiarize themselves with the issue and thus the low priority they have given it. Human rights NGOs have campaigned against specific Bank-sponsored projects, but they have been reluctant to lobby the Bank on human rights on the macro or policy level. According to David Kinley, a professor of inter-

national law who has conducted several studies on the World Bank, the limited NGO activity on human rights could be due to a number of factors:
"It appeared that the critics were either unaware of the relevance of human
rights standards, or they considered that the employment of such language
was less likely to be effective against the Bank than specifically economic,
social or environmental criticisms, possibly because they anticipated resistance on the Bank's part to human rights arguments" (Kinley 2009, 127).
NGOs may also be reluctant to invest limited resources on an agenda they
themselves are internally divided over.

NGOs have been split not only on how to operationalize human rights
at the Bank but also on whether to even advocate for this issue in the first
place. One participant commented:

> We're at the same time very cognizant and nervous that if the Bank . . . were
> to push or be pushed strongly into dealing with human rights, there's a great
> risk of it becoming more than what people bargained for. That's the way that
> these things develop at the Bank. The analogy [is] with the environment.
> People were nudging and fighting the Bank to just not destroy large ecosys-
> tems through their dam-building and road-building. Fifteen years later, to
> have the Bank be the leading financer of environment projects in the world,
> it's like, "Whoa, wait a minute. Now it's the Environment Bank." Is that what
> we wanted? Not necessarily, because [the Bank] approaches things in a very
> particular way. And the distribution of power at the Bank is unequal. And
> there could be a lot of misuse of human rights issues. So there [are] a lot of
> risks. So we're kind of in that middle ground, where we certainly recognize
> that the Bank has significant impacts in many of its operations on human
> rights, in the attainment or realization of human rights. And it needs to rec-
> ognize that. It needs to recognize the obligations. But then we're nervous
> about where it goes from there.[13]

Many civil society advocates are afraid that if the Bank were to work more
directly on human rights, it would co-opt the issue, as they perceive it has
done with the environment.

When NGOs launched earlier campaigns, they were more trusting that
the Bank's gestures for civil society participation would result in desired
reforms. Their experience on the environment changed that perception, as
they watched the Bank transform itself into an institution of "green neo-

liberalism" (Goldman 2005, 154–55). Michael Goldman describes how "the Bank's form of environmental knowledge production has rapidly become hegemonic, disarming and absorbing many of its critics, expanding its terrain of influence, and effectively enlarging the scope and power of its neoliberal agenda" (180). In this way, the Bank may be engaging in a politics of silencing critics by asserting authority over reform agendas such as the environment and "converting the substance of criticisms leveled by social movements into opportunities for the construction and deployment of knowledge in general" (Rajagopal 2003, 126). When the Bank adopts a new agenda, it devotes significant resources to becoming the authoritative source of knowledge on that issue, for example by developing tools, gathering data, writing reports, and training professionals in borrower countries. By doing so, the institution becomes the international arbiter for how such agendas are defined and implemented.

Even though a number of NGOs regret that the Bank has become an authority on environmental issues, several prominent environmental NGOs have nonetheless continued to support the Bank's work in this area. For instance, the World Wildlife Fund (WWF), the Nature Conservancy, and the International Union for Conservation of Nature have forged partnerships with the Bank and even become subcontractors for Bank projects (Goldman 2005). In 2000, the WWF founded the Center for Conservation Finance, which works with Wall Street firms to develop financial instruments that raise capital for conservation, such as environmental investment funds, conservation easements, and trading systems. By presenting its work in the form of business plans, the center operates "through the discourse of financial investments, with biodiversity mapped as investment portfolios and ecosystems measured, evaluated, and valorized for their natural capital and ecological services" (217). This suggests a liberal incoherence among NGOs: civil society is becoming vulnerable to market forces and slowly privatized, thus functioning as "'Trojan horses for global neoliberalism'" (Harvey 2005, 177, quoting Wallace 2003). In fact, there is a growing market for Bank-trained professionals with expertise in neoliberal forms of public-sector privatization and experience in civil society advocacy, who form part of a transnational policy network around development (Goldman 2005). Those NGOs that refuse to follow this trend of privatization have less access to the Bank and arguably less opportunity to influence projects.

In addition to their concerns that the Bank would co-opt the human rights agenda as it has done with the environment, some NGOs are fearful that if an inadequate human rights policy were passed at the Bank, it would take significant effort and likely many years to campaign for any revision. (The revision process for the Bank's indigenous peoples policy lasted more than seven years, and advocates were still unhappy with the revised policy.) In the meantime, the Bank's new policy may then become a ceiling for other international organizations, rather than those organizations being held to higher standards that are being advocated by NGOs. Other multilateral development banks (e.g., the Inter-American Development Bank, the Asian Development Bank, and the African Development Bank) frequently follow the Bank's lead in how they frame issues and design their own policies. Civil society organizations are therefore wary of embarking on another campaign against the Bank that may again result in an unsatisfactory policy, in the World Bank and in other organizations as well. Moreover, even if the policy were satisfactory, there may be substantial underimplementation by Bank employees, as has been the case with other safeguard policies.

Not only is there a lack of consensus among advocates over whether to pressure the Bank to adopt a human rights agenda, but there is also a strong unwillingness on the part of many advocates to reach out to Bank staff to forge an internal-external alliance. NGOs have successfully allied with internal Bank dissidents in the past, as with the campaign to cancel the loan for Nepal's Arun III Hydroelectric Dam in the 1990s (Fox and Brown 1998). But during the past decade, many NGOs became disenchanted with the Bank over failed reforms and the strained and protracted process of revising operational policies, which left many advocates frustrated with their former partners at the Bank. I noticed antagonism toward Bank staff among the workshop participants and a strong preference for creating an external accountability mechanism rather than an internal one. According to many of the participants, the Bank's prior attempts to reach out to civil society have been insincere, arrogant, and not truly collaborative. Whereas the Bank has hired several vocal critics and created a Civil Society Team to reach out to external groups, this may be an attempt to control critique and make superficial changes without actually adopting substantial reforms. Moreover, the Civil Society Team lacks financial independence from the Bank and accountability to NGO constituencies.

The hostility among some NGOs toward Bank staff members has made it difficult for internal advocates to mobilize external support for their recent efforts to introduce a human rights agenda. Prior successful campaigns for Bank reform have featured "the reciprocal interaction between external critics and internal Bank dissidents" (Fox and Brown 1998, 4). The impact of NGO advocacy is correlated with efforts to reach out to influential insider allies, who in turn become further empowered and legitimated by external pressure (ibid.). Yet given their dissatisfaction with prior reforms generated by their alliances with Bank staff, NGOs have lost trust in this strategy and are seeking alternative avenues for effecting change.

Internal Pressure

Over the past two decades, internal advocates have been more active than external ones in pressuring Bank management to adopt a human rights agenda. Various individuals and factions have attempted to do so through multiple mechanisms but faced a number of institutional obstacles. I will briefly review the history of internal campaigns to introduce human rights into the Bank's work. In particular, I highlight how various actors or groups campaigned for human rights in different ways, set different goals, and faced different types of obstacles. My discussion is based on archival research and personal interviews with retired and current Bank employees. The internal advocates did not generate enough momentum (certainly nothing close to an internal social movement), and the factions were often plagued by internal divisions that stemmed from employees' disciplinary backgrounds. In addition, they suffered from a lack of resources and failed to mobilize external support for their internal campaigns.

Early to Mid-1990s

From my interviews with former and current employees familiar with the human-rights-related activities of the Bank, I conclude that the first internal efforts to integrate human rights norms into the Bank's operational work occurred in the early 1990s. This initiative was led by an interdisciplinary working group of operational staff from the African region, who framed it in the context of a new institutional focus on governance as a key ingredient for development (see World Bank 1989, 60–61). Members of the group included employees of various disciplines who worked in Africa. Given the prevailing view at the Bank that human rights work bumped up against the political prohibition in its Articles of Agreement,[14] the working group aimed to convince Bank officials that human rights is an underlying factor in achieving good governance.

To do so, the group organized several brown-bag lunches, workshops, and symposiums on the relationship among human rights, governance, and participation. Given a project-level focus, the working group primarily addressed country officers who could potentially integrate civil and political rights (including the rule of law and freedom of association) in their dialogues with government officials. According to one leading member of the working group, the link among gender, development, and human rights was also an important priority:

> The women's rights issue and the arguable lack of attention in the human rights community to women's rights is an important piece of this puzzle. The human rights community is out there, and nobody will deny that women's rights is human rights. But in reality, you have two completely separate groups of people working on this. So we were trying with the Africa region of the Bank to bring out this set of connections with women's rights. Women are perceived as minors legally. They do not have separate rights, [and] there's a whole set of cultural and related concerns about women's rights. . . . So all of this stuff about legal rights, legal protections, access to legal services, the gender responsiveness of laws, the whole set of connections between gender violence, sexual violence, HIV/AIDS, property rights, business rights for women. All of these we would see as rights issues that are relevant for development and growth in Africa.[15]

In advocating for the Bank to address human rights issues, the group invoked recent legal opinions by then general counsel Ibrahim Shihata, who had written that "political events which have a bearing on the economic conditions of a member or on the member's ability to implement a project or the Bank's ability to supervise a project may be taken into consideration by the Board" (Shihata 1988, 12). Shihata's opinions lent support to the working group's position that human rights is a legitimate and important concern for the Bank and should not be dismissed as being too "political."

The group succeeded in bringing attention to the issue in the early 1990s, but it became inoperative in the middle to late 1990s soon after James

Wolfensohn took office as president. The reasons for the working group's decline were primarily contingent. Many of the group members were diverted by their work on governance and corruption, which had become priorities at the institution. According to one of the most active working group members, it was difficult to motivate employees to care about human rights when they were preoccupied with the technocratic aspects of their jobs:

> Most people in the Bank are technocratic people—doing their operational stuff, working on projects, doing investments, doing standard economic analyses. We are, for the most part, technocrats. Most people probably don't spend a whole lot of time, even if we're card-carrying members of Amnesty International, . . . necessarily thinking about the ways in which human rights do or do not affect what we do.[16]

In addition, some of the senior officials who had previously supported the working group retired or moved to other departments. Without support from senior staff, the members of the working group could not easily invest time and resources in promoting human rights research and education. This state of affairs changed by the late 1990s.

Late 1990s–2004

In 1995, James Wolfensohn became president of the Bank and ushered in an era of more open dialogue on human rights. Wolfensohn was responding to the external pressure that had been building on the Bank and other development agencies, and to his personal conviction to bring more attention to the social dimensions of development. According to Wolfensohn, it took about three or four years to impress upon the staff that human rights was an important issue within the context of the Bank's work:

> I was interested in human rights from day one. But what you find when you're running an organization is that you can't give an immediate instruction and say this is now the direction that ten thousand people in a hundred countries move [in]. You have to prepare the ground. You have to get people to think about it. You have to get them to warm up to the idea.[17]

Admittedly, Wolfensohn did not succeed in creating a human rights consciousness among staff. But under his leadership, the Bank published its first official report on the subject, which recognized the institution's role in promoting and protecting human rights but stopped short of stating that it had an international legal obligation to do so (World Bank 1998). Since the publication of the report in 1998, documents issued by the Bank and speeches by officials have periodically mentioned human rights, although the Board of Executive Directors has continued to oppose their official incorporation into institutional policy. Wolfensohn recognized the unlikelihood of getting the board to spearhead a human rights agenda since it was and remains deeply divided over the issue. Instead of consulting with board members, Wolfensohn and senior management appealed to employees in an effort to first build support within the institution.

The momentum for a human rights strategy began in 2002. On May 2 of that year, the Bank organized an all-day internal workshop entitled "Human Rights and Sustainable Development: What Role for the Bank?" which was attended by about a hundred employees from across the institution and featured the chair of the UN Committee on Economic, Social and Cultural Rights as a guest speaker. The purpose of the workshop was to increase the staff members' awareness of human rights and to discuss possible implications for the Bank's operations. Wolfensohn announced in a plenary address that the Bank had approached human rights in a "step-by-step way, doing it quietly, trying to assert the delivery of rights, but not necessarily couching it in the terms of human rights."[18] He indicated that the mood was changing and that it was time to take the words *human rights* out of the closet.[19]

Soon thereafter, Wolfensohn invited a few senior staff members to lead an institutionwide task force on human rights and draft a strategy paper that he could present at the Bank's next annual meetings.[20] Coordinated by the Social Development Department, the task force included staff from the Legal, Human Development, External Affairs, Sustainable Development, and Poverty Reduction Departments. Involving representatives from a variety of departments was a critical step since it allowed cross-disciplinary dialogue and prevented one department from co-opting the agenda.

One of the leaders of the task force was Judith Edstrom, the sector manager of the Social Development Department, who had a background in education and field experience in Africa. As the Bank's focal point at the UN's Commission for Social Development, Edstrom had worked with other UN agencies to draft a set of guidelines called *Principles and Good Practice in Social Policy*, which was published by the Bank's Development

Committee in April 1999. The guidelines draw on the Copenhagen Declaration and Program of Action, developed at the World Summit for Social Development in 1995.[21] They affirm the institution's role in "distill[ing] lessons of good practice to assist its members to draw upon [it] in support of their economic and social development goals" (World Bank 1999, 2). They also note trade-offs that may arise in implementation of the outlined principles. Following the model of the UN guidelines, Edstrom and the other Social Development Department representatives in the task force advocated for a principles-based approach to human rights that would focus on ethics and social policy goals rather than legal standards. They thought that a "common sense approach" avoiding a formal legalistic interpretation would accord staff greater flexibility in operationalizing human-rights-related principles.[22] A normative framework based on human dignity would emphasize ethical considerations as opposed to legal obligations, under the presumption that board members would perceive such an approach as less "political" and less of a threat to their sovereignty.

Another prominent member of the task force was Alfredo Sfeir-Younis, who later became the Bank's focal point on human rights. As an economist and former special representative of the Bank to the World Trade Organization and the UN, Sfeir-Younis had developed a unique ability to bridge the discourses of economic development and human rights, which he viewed as mutually reinforcing frameworks. He focused on the need to "humanize economics" and locate human rights within a new economic development paradigm, rather than just treating it as a legal issue.[23] Though he strived to create institutional space to debate the role of human rights within the Bank, his efforts were never fully realized, as I describe below.

The task force members met over the next year with regional and network vice presidents as they prepared a background report on human rights. They presented the report to the board's Committee on Development Effectiveness in June 2003, at a meeting chaired by then-managing director Shengman Zhang. The report reviewed the Bank's existing work in support of human rights. It also identified the difficulties of the institution adopting a human rights approach, including the need to avoid being the world's human rights policeman (notwithstanding the Bank's role as an economic policeman); and the view that human rights is too vague, legalistic, and categorical a concept and is therefore not amenable to a pragmatic approach.[24]

Citing legal restrictions in the Articles of Agreement, the report questioned whether it was the Bank's niche to work on human rights, particularly when other international organizations such as the United Nations have a greater competency and mandate to do so.[25] These rationalizations demonstrate that the Bank's senior management remained cautious about investing in a human rights agenda, partly due to fears of the board's likely disapproval.

The committee ultimately did not approve the report because it did not feel ready to address such a controversial issue.[26] According to one task force member, although senior officials had reviewed multiple drafts they just "got cold feet" about endorsing a paper on human rights and began to "backpedal" by calling for more background studies and analysis before progressing any further on a strategy.[27] Following the committee's meeting, Wolfensohn assigned the human rights portfolio to a managing director in charge of the Human Development Network, Mamphela Ramphele, a South African doctor and social anthropologist and one of the founders of the Black Consciousness Movement. Sfeir-Younis was appointed as her senior advisor on a number of issues including human rights.[28] Wolfensohn's decision to upgrade the human rights portfolio to a managing director was influenced by recent activity at the IFC, whose Executive Vice President Peter Woicke had recently announced his support for adoption of human rights criteria in loan decisions (see Sevastopulo 2003), and the IFC already had two dedicated staff members working on the issue. As a result, NGOs such as Human Rights Watch were pressuring the Bank to evaluate its position on human rights in light of that of the IFC.[29]

During the fall of 2003 and early 2004, Ramphele and Sfeir-Younis chaired several meetings on human rights with senior officers and asked the regional vice presidents in operations to identify human rights focal points. This effort was part of a decentralized strategy, with regions left to determine how they would prefer to tackle the issue. Some regions did not follow up on this request, while others, such as the South Asia and the Europe and Central Asia (ECA) units, decided to conduct stock-taking exercises of their activities related to human rights. I am closely aware of this process because I served as one of ECA's human rights focal points along with a young staff lawyer who worked in ECA's Social Development Department.[30] We prepared a report that assessed the region's contribution to human rights, based on a systematic review of the project portfolio and relevant documents, as well as semistructured interviews with staff. Although we submitted the report to the regional vice president in March 2004 and expected to participate subsequently in a learning exercise to communicate our results, none of the promised follow-up occurred. Moreover, there was little coordination across regions, with Ramphele and Sfeir-Younis having chaired only a few meetings with the focal points and vice presidents.

This phase of internal human rights advocacy reached a crescendo in March 2004.[31] As mentioned earlier, the UN and NYU School of Law convened a conference entitled "Human Rights and Development: Towards Mutual Reinforcement" (see Alston and Robinson 2005). The conference featured a keynote address by Wolfensohn and presentations by several senior officials, including the recently appointed general counsel, Roberto Dañino, who outlined what would later become a legal opinion on human rights. But the momentum seemed to stop soon thereafter. Aside from the publication of a book based on the conference, there was no substantive follow-up and the Bank did not invest additional resources toward continuing the initiative. In addition, Ramphele resigned from the Bank in April 2004, and then Sfeir-Younis departed within the next year. Reasons for Ramphele's departure included her dissatisfaction with the amount of authority she was given as managing director, her inability to master the inner workings and power politics within an institution where she had never previously worked, and her desire to return to South Africa to effect more grassroots change.

Reasons for Failure

In view of the flurry of activity over human rights between 2002 and 2004, many key ingredients for the adoption of human rights norms and their eventual internalization seem to have been in place: support from the president for development of a strategy that would be presented to the board; appointment of a managing director to oversee the human rights portfolio; and formation of an interdisciplinary task force composed of representatives from different departments. Why, then, did the task force and the Ramphele-led initiative not succeed in gathering internal support and pushing through a strategy on human rights for the Bank? I first describe the institutional reasons for the failure of internal efforts. I then analyze the broader historical cause in which these institutional factors are rooted: ambivalence over the conflicting relationship between human rights and the prevailing neoliberal ideology within the Bank.

Those familiar with the events, including several members of the task force, cite various organizational reasons for its failure and that of the region-based initiative to capitalize on the growing momentum toward adopting human rights norms. These reasons include excessive caution and backpedaling on the part of senior management and the board's Committee on Development Effectiveness, internal resistance to collaborating with civil society organizations, and failure to invest sufficient resources to carry out the requisite activities for increasing staff awareness of human rights. Task members seemed supportive of the principles but cautious about putting them into practice since they were not given a clear mandate from the president and board. Without strong support from the leadership to prioritize this issue and implement it in the Bank's day-to-day operations, the task force members made only symbolic gestures rather than concrete steps toward change.

Wolfensohn himself admitted he should have placed more emphasis on human rights during his tenure:

> The thing that I thought I had done was to establish the issue of human rights as being an important issue for people at the Bank. If I didn't go far enough, then I made a mistake probably by not getting an explicit policy passed by the board. . . . Maybe in retrospect, I should've made a bigger deal of it and tried to put it within the context of some legal framework or some administrative framework. At the time, it didn't occur to me to do that. . . . Maybe I should've done more to give it definition and purpose.[32]

It is unclear, however, whether bringing a human rights policy before the board would have been effective at that time, given the unlikelihood of approval and the disagreements among staff over what such a policy would entail.

Moreover, some criticized the leaders of the task force for being too theoretical and for having underemphasized the concrete practical steps that were needed to push the agenda forward.[33] They mentioned that Sfeir-Younis's mandate as senior advisor was unclear, so he did not have enough space and resources to pursue the issue effectively.[34] Others thought that Ramphele lacked the political capital and Bank experience to influence senior management. Even though she was a managing director, many employ-ees considered her an outsider since she had only recently joined the Bank (in 2000), and they viewed her as having lower status than the two other managing directors because she was responsible for "soft" issues such as hu-man development.[35]

In addition to the reasons stated above, the most significant institu-tional factor behind the failure of the internal efforts between 2002 and 2004 may have been a clash of expertise. Task force members complained of the difficulty of reaching a consensus among employees from different sectors and disciplinary backgrounds, who held divergent views on how to define human rights and interpret them with respect to Bank operations. The theoretically oriented members (like Sfeir-Younis, who emphasized the indivisibility of human rights) clashed with the more pragmatically minded, who were mainly concerned with operational issues and the need to make trade-offs among rights and other goals in projects with limited budgets. One employee familiar with the events noted that the failure to bring about a human rights strategy was not due to resistance from the board or se-nior management but rather "turf battles and just the difficulty of doing something like this in such a multi-sectoral organization."[36] Amid internal disputes, the task force failed to build a constituency of staff members in support of its mission.

The task force also did not succeed in mobilizing external support for its internal campaign. Intraorganizational social movements often arise with support from extraorganizational movements (Strang and Jung 2005). Although some of the task force members had ties to external advocates, they did not attempt to generate a unified effort with civil society represen-tatives but focused instead on internal activities. In addition, as mentioned earlier, the NGOs themselves were not united in their lobbying efforts and did not pursue alliances with staff.

The final missing ingredient was support by the Legal Department. This is surprising given the centrality of the Articles of Agreement to determin-ing the Bank's role with respect to human rights. Although the task force included a lawyer from the department, he did not consult with the general counsel and did not consider himself the department's official representative on human rights. Other members of the Legal Department felt shut out from the process by task force members, which was certainly a valid criticism.[37] In the fall of 2003, when Ramphele and Sfeir-Younis were leading the decentralized strategy with region-based focal points, the Legal Department was only belatedly included in the discussions and was not regularly consulted.

Finally, turf wars erupted between the Legal Department and the regional departments, which wanted to retain control of the human rights agenda and not cede it to the lawyers. As one of the human rights focal points for the Europe and Central Asia region, I observed how the Social Development Department and the Legal Department were jockeying to assert their jurisdiction over this controversial issue. A lawyer whom I knew who worked under the general counsel had asked me for a copy of the report on human rights that I had been working on. When I asked permission from my supervisor in Social Development, I was sternly instructed not to share the report with employees in the Legal Department for fear that they would co-opt the agenda and push for an overly legalistic interpretation of human rights. It literally took weeks for the lawyer to eventually obtain a copy of the report, which she did by asking the general counsel to directly request it from a senior official in the ECA region. This experience demonstrated how turf wars impeded the development of a unified strategy for human rights.

The distrust between members of the Legal and Social Development Departments stems from tension over what is considered of value toward the Bank's goals and how development success is defined. Most of the lawyers in the Legal Department are transactional specialists who work on loan agreements. A senior counsel at the Bank observed, "We tend to be more conservative. We tend to really uphold the policies on the book, rather than . . . [those in the regional operations units] because they need to adapt different projects to different situations"[38] There are certainly a variety of perspectives among Bank lawyers, but their knowledge system in general is rule-based and emphasizes universal knowledge over contextual. In contrast, the knowledge system of employees within the Social Development Department (who are largely sociologists and anthropologists) focuses on the contingencies of practice rather than policy rationality (Mosse 2004b). These employees also prioritize adaptation to local knowledge and recognition of the spectrum of social variables that shape development (Cernea 1996). In this way, they express a "high degree of self-criticism and skepticism regarding official narratives and development recipes" (Mosse 2004b, 80). In fact, one of the first anthropologists who joined the Bank in the mid-1970s remarked that "intellectual combat has been part of the history of anthropological work in the Bank, and it continues to be so—a creative struggle of ideas, interpretations, and models" (Cernea 1996, 15).

The battlefield between knowledge systems has translated into mistrust between the departments as well as differences in policy formulation. Even though dissension between the departments continued, the Legal Department's role in discussions over human rights expanded after the appointment of general counsel Dañino in late 2003. As the next chapter details, Dañino championed the human rights agenda over the next two years and paved the way for recent efforts in that regard by members of the Legal Department.

Staff largely cited institutional reasons for the failure of internal campaigns (including turf wars, a failure to form external alliances, and a clash of expertise, among others), but these organizational factors are symptoms of an underlying cause related to the cultural history of the Bank—namely, ambivalence within the Bank's apolitical image and neoliberal ideology over the issue of human rights. Though members of senior management took significant steps to push the agenda forward, their actions were hesitant and tentative because of their anxieties over the undetermined role of human rights. Even the way in which the internal campaign ended was ambivalent; it quietly died rather than being flatly rejected or officially dismantled.

The uncertainty over human rights within the Bank reflects internal contradictions at the core of neoliberal capitalism:

> The fact that it appears both to include and to marginalize in unanticipated ways; to produce desire and expectation on a global scale, yet to decrease the certainty of work or the security of persons; to magnify class differences but to undercut class consciousness; above all, to offer up vast, almost instantaneous riches to those who master its spectral technologies—and simultaneously, to threaten the very existence of those who do not [Comaroff and Comaroff 2000, 298].

These tensions are apparent in the simultaneous embrace of and opposition to human rights within neoliberal ideology:

> The relationship between the realization of human rights and the ideological orientation of neoliberal globalization is ambiguous in conception and behavioral effects. To the extent that neoliberal perspectives are antiauthori-

tarian, they tend to encourage the implementation of human rights in state-society relations, especially through the argument that economic develop-ment will be frustrated if such rights are not upheld. However, the neoliberal outlook ruptures a sense of human solidarity within a given political commu-nity, and effectively rejects any commitment of responsibility to those mem-bers who are economically and socially disadvantaged [Falk 2000, 48–49].

Treating the individual as the foundation for economic and political life, neoliberal ideology is consistent with individual freedoms and certain hu-man rights such as property rights. At the same time, it does not support those rights that promote social egalitarian objectives such as distributive justice. According to David Harvey, "Neoliberal concern for the individual trumps any social democratic concern for equality, democracy, and social solidarities" (2005, 176). Neoliberalism supports individual free choice, but it is suspicious of democratic governance as a potential threat to individual rights. It also opposes such strong collective institutions as trade unions and other forms of social solidarity that restrain capital accumulation. Harvey notes that, "faced with social movements that seek collective interventions, . . . the neoliberal state is itself forced to intervene, sometimes repressively, thus denying the very freedoms it is supposed to uphold" (69). Similarly, the more neoliberalism moves toward authoritarianism in market enforce-ment, the more it threatens the ideals of individual freedom that in theory it should promote.

We see these internal contradictions in the gap between the Bank's rhet-oric (which promotes poverty reduction and affirms the link between de-velopment and human rights) and practices that have at times resulted in displaced indigenous communities and environmental degradation. Bank projects aim to improve social welfare in the aggregate but do not evaluate the distribution of costs among individuals and communities. The Bank's support for human rights has been selective, varying with the rights, the sector, and the country where the Bank is lending money. For instance, ac-cording to the director of an international organization for trade unions, the Bank has been inconsistent in support for core labor standards:

The response we get from the Bank is that freedom of association and the right to collective bargaining are political issues. And the others are not. And I've found that totally implausible. Forced labor is not a political issue? Discrimination against women is not a political issue? . . . [Bank officials] said that allowing for trade unions is a distortion of the free market and potentially could harm growth. . . . Well, if your job is poverty reduction and you have a standard [like freedom of association] that doesn't harm growth but does make for more equal distribution of income, and therefore should reduce poverty, you don't need any more arguments than that.[39]

The Bank is thus hiding behind its seemingly apolitical image when refusing to support the rights to collective bargaining and free association, yet it concurrently respects other core labor rights (antislavery, antichild labor, and antidiscrimination) that are more consistent with neoliberal ideology.

Conversations with Bank employees also reflect an ambivalence over the institution's role in promoting human rights. These quotes all come from one employee during a single interview:

I'm personally extremely troubled, particularly about freedom of association not being discussed as a right because about two hundred unionists are shot every year. . . . I wish we could've used more of that language. . . .

Yeah, the way that [then President] Wolfensohn would put it: "We don't call it human rights, but it is." [But] coming at it starting from a human rights perspective actually changes your work, so I think it's bullshit. . . .

The job of most people at the institution is to help governments deliver on specific policy goals that we've pretended are not political and not related to human rights. And everyone's willing to pretend this because we think we could get further. . . . And also because it is a bank lending money that has to show a return in order for them to pay it back. If it were the UN, it's different. Of course, the UN can go in talking about human rights. . . .

People are actually doing human rights work here. I mean, we are actually helping draft a constitution that includes strong gender equality language, and things like that. So there is the stuff where we say we're getting human rights through the back door kind of stuff. But that's kind of a lame way to describe it. And then there's the direct human rights work that we do. There's direct capacity building of press and direct human rights work in terms of nondiscrimination in AIDS and gender. But it's a far cry from a rights-based development approach, like the UNDP.

[Human rights] is sometimes a useful lens for us. I don't think we're taking advantage of it as much. But we also have to keep in mind this loan element that we cannot sacrifice: the economic rigor. And I don't think it necessarily has to, but the economics and human rights literature empirically is not super strong. It's pretty weak. So it's pretty irresponsible to be lending money if you haven't done the rigorous economic analysis.[40]

The employee quoted here recognizes the Bank's human-rights-related work and reiterates common arguments for why the Bank should not adopt a rights-based approach, for example, that the organization is a lending bank after all and not the UN, so such an approach may sacrifice its economic rigor. At the same time, she acknowledges the inconsistencies in Bank practice (including staff "pretending" that certain policy goals are not political) and criticizes former President Wolfensohn's rhetorical support for the issue. What we see here is that the cultural logics of the Bank's dominant neoliberal ideology with respect to human rights constrain how employees think and talk about the issue. That employees reinforce this ambiguous stance further affirms the Bank's identity as an institution that is simultaneously apolitical in image yet deeply political in practice.

Conclusion

Organizational change frequently occurs when there is concurrent internal and external pressure. In the case of the Bank, the pressure has not successfully incited the institution to address human rights explicitly and directly. It is likely that external pressure from other bilateral and multilateral agencies, the IFC, and the private sector has pushed the Bank to reexamine its approach, although not to significantly alter it. Since the Bank prides itself on setting global standards on development issues, one would have expected it to become a leader in human rights policy making, especially given competitive pressures from public and private institutions. This has not yet occurred. It is also surprising that internal efforts by employees have not produced substantive changes in Bank policy toward human rights. Turf wars and the failure to form alliances with external advocates are among the institutional symptoms of the failure of internal campaigns. Yet the underlying cause is an ambivalence over human rights within the neoliberal ideology that is dominant within the institution.

In the following chapters, I continue the story of *why* human rights has remained marginal despite what we might have predicted. Although political and legal constraints partly account for this phenomenon, it is necessary to analyze the bureaucratic obstacles—and in particular, a clash of expertise among staff—that have limited the diffusion of human rights norms within the organization.

Chapter 2

Political and Legal Constraints

*The Board of Executive Directors
and the Articles of Agreement*

W HY HASN'T THE BANK adopted a human rights agenda despite internal and external pressure over the past two decades? Many scholars, policy makers, and advocates have addressed this question, and their responses often focus on two types of obstacles to human rights adoption: political and legal (see, e.g., Darrow 2003; Skogly 2001). The political constraints stem from opposition by certain member countries and internal conflict within the Bank's Board of Executive Directors. The legal constraints refer to restrictions in the institution's Articles of Agreement, or founding constitution. Both factors have certainly influenced the Bank's approach to human rights. Even though they remain notable obstacles, their saliency has dwindled over time. What are underemphasized are the institutional factors, including the Bank's incentive system and a clash of expertise among staff, which I address in Chapter 3. I focus this chapter on the political and legal constraints and why they are not as significant as one would expect.

The Board of Executive Directors

One of the most commonly cited reasons for the marginality of human rights at the Bank is political resistance by members of its Board of Executive Directors. The board is composed of twenty-four executive directors who represent countries or country groups. The directors serve in their capacity as individuals rather than as country ambassadors and, as officials of the Bank, are paid by the institution. Five executive directors are appointed from the five donor countries that contribute the largest number of shares—currently, France, Germany, Japan, the United Kingdom, and the United States. The other nineteen directors are elected by regional groups of the other member countries. Unlike the UN, where each country gets one vote, the Bank links voting power to members' capital subscriptions, which are based on a country's relative economic strength. Therefore, the Bank's governance structure is undemocratic as it correlates power with capital and reproduces colonial relationships between poorer and richer countries in the name of development.

In practice, the Bank is largely dominated by a few donor countries, with the United States yielding the most leverage and historically selecting the Bank's president (see Weaver 2008, 50–57). In addition, Ngaire Woods notes: "More than three-quarters of the members of each of the IMF and the World Bank are not directly represented on the Board of Executive Directors. Nor are they represented in the senior management of either institution. Many have virtually no nationals working on the staff. These are the countries who are most deeply affected by each of the institutions" (Woods 2006, 190).

Certain borrower countries do yield significant influence. A considerable amount of the Bank's annual net income derives from its largest clients, including China, India, and Brazil. These middle-income countries can threaten to default on their loans or resist unfavorable conditions during loan negotiations (Weaver 2008). Moreover, increased competition from the private sector and from domestic and regional development agencies furthers the Bank's dependence on these middle-income countries.

Power politics among member countries shapes decision making over which projects are approved, whether to place conditionalities on borrower countries, and which policies the Bank promotes and applies in practice. Moreover, the states are the primary means through which development projects are implemented and Bank-sponsored economic and social policies are enforced. For example, a community-based education project for indigenous peoples must be mediated through the state where it is based before reaching any intended beneficiaries. Because the Bank signs loan and credit agreements with states, they are the agents primarily responsible for project implementation. As part of a loan agreement, a borrower country may be required to adopt and implement a resettlement action plan designed in accordance with the Bank's operational policy on involuntary resettlement. By conditioning loans on compliance with operational poli cies, the Bank plays a crucial role in affecting the behavior and institutional framework of borrower countries. A country's breach of a loan agreement gives the Bank reason to suspend disbursements, although such a threat rarely materializes. Instead, the Bank may limit involvement in future projects in the country for fear of further noncompliance with Bank policies (Kingsbury 1999, 338–39).

Member countries govern the Bank through the Board of Governors, which includes one governor per member country (often the minister of finance or minister of development) and meets once a year at the Bank's annual meetings. Under the Articles of Agreement, the Board of Governors has delegated day-to-day decision making power to the Board of Executive Directors, which serves as the Bank's policy making organ while the president and senior management are responsible for operational, administrative, and organizational issues. The Board of Executive Directors meets once or twice a week to vote on loan and credit proposals and make decisions on strategic and policy items, including the administrative budget. Yet it has very rarely exercised the power to reject loans proposed by management. Executive directors trust that staff members have already vetted projects to ensure they are technically and financially sound (Caufield 1996). My study of the Bank's internal decision-making process confirmed that employees can operate quite independently from the board and have even carried out certain sensitive management issues without board approval or involvement.

An institutional constraint that favors agency autonomy is the short time horizon of board members, compared to that of the Bank president. Most executive directors serve for just one or two two-year terms, whereas the president's tenure can amount to five years, or more if he or she is reelected. Roughly a third of the board members change every year. As a result, the directors' knowledge of the history and practice of the institution is quite narrow.[1] According to former director Moisés Naím, in an interview with Catherine Caufield, "It is impossible, even for the few of them that have a good prior understanding of the institution, to master the overwhelming array of complex issues on which they are supposed to develop an independent opinion" (1996, 239). Naím further explains that the directors end up relying on the guidance of management because they are "no match for a usually brilliant group of professionals with decades of experience at the Bank" (ibid.).

Given the differing time horizons of the president and the executive directors, the president can incrementally introduce organizational changes that are not perceived as too radical by board members, who are constrained by their limited institutional memory and inability to exert effective oversight of the president. Former President James Wolfensohn adopted an incremental strategy for introducing reforms during his second five-year term. By then, he had served at the Bank longer than any board member and could get a lot more done in comparison to the achievements of his first few years in office. Wolfensohn treated the board in this manner:

> If you make the assumption to the board that this is the way you operate, you very rarely get challenged. . . . So if you can proceed in the institution with a set of assumptions that you are doing things in the way they should be done, . . . you can incrementally do a tremendous amount. Because it's unlikely that anyone will challenge you. Because they think that maybe this is the way the Bank should operate. So I got a lot of things done incrementally without coming to the board for big policy decisions. I knew that if I went to the board on many of the policy decisions, [I'd] run into a hell of a lot of problems.[2]

Wolfensohn adopted this incremental strategy to advance his anticorruption agenda. He noted that by the time he left, he was spending about $6–7 million a year on corruption, although he had never presented a policy to the board.[3]

Another important reason for the board's lack of significant power over the Bank's management and staff is that by tradition it operates by "consensus" when a formal vote is taken, according to senior management. In fact, formal voting is infrequent; most of the real negotiations occur during informal meetings where individual executive directors from powerful countries voice their support or opposition to a proposed agenda item. The board represents itself as making decisions unanimously in order to mask the hegemonic influence of the largest donor countries. It is also a tactic used by senior officials to stem criticism from advocates and deflect responsibility to a highly opaque body that is inaccessible to outsiders (e.g., neither transcripts nor minutes of board meetings are disclosed). Such was the experience of a labor rights activist who repeatedly tried to put core labor standards on the Bank's agenda: "[Then President] Wolfensohn told us in the last high-level meetings that he himself is in favor of making [core labor standards] a condition of all loans, but he said that it would never pass the board. The thing is that they've never done the debate at the board; they've never actually proposed it. And there's a number that would in fact support it."[4] Similarly, senior management frequently blames the board for inaction over the human rights agenda.

Historically, the board has been deeply divided over the issue of human rights. Some member states, such as China and Saudi Arabia, strongly oppose an explicit human rights agenda that would include the protection of civil and political rights (which they view as a reflection of "Western" values). Others, such as India and Brazil (middle-income countries responsible for a substantial portion of the Bank's revenue), fear that human rights would increase transaction costs for loans by requiring expensive and time-consuming safeguards. Another reason for their opposition is their view that a human rights agenda would encroach on their sovereignty and turn the institution into a human rights enforcer. Some countries fear the Bank may condition loans on meeting human rights standards and thereby serve as the arbiter for what is considered acceptable state behavior. This type of conditionality would adversely affect borrower countries with poor human rights records while not having an impact on donor countries with similar records. Among countries that moderately support a human rights agenda, there is disagreement over what it might look like: Should the Bank adopt a rights-based approach to development? A human rights operational policy? A human rights assessment that would limit the possibility of projects causing human rights violations? The diversity of the board makes it difficult to agree on a single approach. Because the board operates by consensus, disagreements on such issues as human rights have simply resulted in inaction.

Bank officials have recognized the unlikelihood of getting board support for a human rights agenda and avoided proposing it because they fear a backlash against the issue if they tried and failed to gain approval. Instead, internal advocates are in favor of an alternative strategy: introducing a sensitive topic such as human rights not through board approval but by making incremental changes in operations. Success in pushing an agenda forward in the Bank thus depends on employees maintaining their autonomy from the board as they exercise discretion over daily operations.

There is one notable exception to the board's limited role in advancing human rights: recent initiatives by the Nordic member states, including circulation of a working paper on the issue to the board and launching of a trust fund to support related activities by Bank staff. (Trust funds do not require board approval.) The Nordic countries likely recognized the difficulty of having the board pass an overarching policy on human rights. They were therefore seeking to fund activities that would incrementally change operational practice and raise the human rights consciousness of employees, who could then push for more permanent changes in Bank policy. This reinforces the view that the deeply divided board is not as critical an obstacle to human rights adoption as it may seem, since some countries and staff have been able to bypass it while attempting to push forward their agenda.

Legal Obstacles

When explaining why the institution has not addressed human rights more openly, Bank officials and scholars have commonly cited legal obstacles that arise out of international law and the Bank's own Articles of Agreement. Here I clarify the uncertainty over the Bank's human rights obligations under international law, and I analyze relevant legal restrictions in the Articles of Agreement that have historically impeded the Bank's direct engagement in human rights.

The Bank's Obligations Under International Law

What does international law say about the Bank's responsibilities with respect to human rights? Does the Bank have an obligation to ensure that its projects, programs, and internal policies conform to international human rights standards, and that its activities do not facilitate human rights abuses? Does it have a responsibility to promote human rights in member states?

To address these questions, the first and most important issue to explore is the extent to which the Bank as an international organization is bound by rules of customary international law beyond the charter, including customary international law norms on human rights. Commentators continue to debate both this question and even what constitutes customary international law on human rights.

The Bank functions as an international body with legal personality due to "the nature of the specific powers granted under [the] Articles (notably the power to conclude agreements governed by international law, and the provisions establishing [its] relationship with other international organizations), entitlement to specified privileges and immunities, and the fact that [it] operate[s] extensively within the international sphere" (Darrow 2003, 126). According to legal scholars, the Bank's status as an international legal person implies its role as both a subject and an object of international responsibilities and obligations, *possibly* including obligations incumbent upon the organization under international agreements and customary international law (see Bradlow 1996, 63; Shihata 1988, 47).

Because international organizations (IOs), unlike states, cannot become parties to treaties, they are not directly bound by human rights treaties. Yet, according to the International Court of Justice, international organizations can be bound by obligations under general principles of international law[5] and are capable of possessing international rights and duties.[6] IOs are also bound by *jus cogens*, peremptory norms of international law such as prohibition of genocide (Schermers 1998). In addition, the Bank has obligations as a specialized agency of the United Nations.[7] The Bank must respect the purposes and principles in the UN Charter, including "the human rights purposes as stated in Article 55, as elaborated in the [Universal Declaration of Human Rights] and the body of international human rights law built upon it" (Darrow 2003, 128). Furthermore, it must have "due regard" for decisions of the UN Security Council, although it is not required to follow the recommendations of the UN specialized human rights agencies (see Skogly 2001; Bradlow 1996).

The second question to ask about the Bank's obligations under international law is whether the institution has any duties vis-à-vis the members. Because only some of the member states are parties to particular human rights agreements, the Bank's responsibilities would vary with respect to different members. Whether the Bank should go as far as enforcing states' treaty obligations through loan conditionalities or assisting states in implementing their treaty obligations through technical assistance remains a matter of debate (Bradlow 2002).

The final issue concerns what role, if any, international financial institutions such as the Bank should play in the progressive development of international law—for example, by promoting human rights in development. Although international conferences, such as the 1993 Vienna World Confer ence on Human Rights and the 2000 Millennium Summit, have recognized the interdependence of human rights and development, the rules of customary international law in this area are still subject to dispute.

In summary, legal scholars have yet to agree on the international legal obligations of the Bank with respect to human rights. The institution has skirted most of these arguments and instead focused on a limited mandate under the Articles of Agreement, whose interpretation has become a locus of contention among Bank staff, advocates, and policy makers.

The Articles of Agreement

Many scholars, policy makers, and advocates have focused on restrictions in the Articles of Agreement that indirectly pertain to human rights. The most relevant legal restrictions arise out of two provisions—Article IV, Section 10; and Article III, Section 5(b)—which place limits on the factors staff members may consider in their decisions.[8] Article IV, Section 10, prohibits political activity and permits only economic considerations in decision making: "The Bank and its officers shall not interfere in the political affairs of any member; nor shall they be influenced in their decisions by the political character of the member or members concerned. Only economic considerations shall be relevant to their decisions, and these considerations shall be weighted impartially in order to achieve the purposes stated in Article I."

Article III, Section 5(b), limits the factors the Bank may consider in granting loans and restricts political considerations: "The Bank shall make arrangements to ensure that the proceeds of any loan are used only for the purposes for which the loan was granted, with due attention to considerations of economy and efficiency and without regard to political or other non-economic influences or considerations."

These provisions have historically stymied the Bank's explicit engagement with human rights, particularly civil and political rights, which have been interpreted as "political considerations." As a result, Bank employees have argued that their work can promote human rights only indirectly.

The antipolitical nature of the Articles of Agreement reflects the history behind the Bank's founding in 1944 and the distribution of responsibility among international organizations. The Bank and the IMF were established at the Bretton Woods conference, which "sought to create mechanisms by which to minimize economic shock and turmoil, and maximize economic growth and stability" (Kinley 2009, 134). Social and humanitarian concerns were not part of the Bank's original mandate but rather were intended to be addressed by the UN, which was soon to be established in 1945 (ibid.). Although this division of responsibilities has become blurred over time, it is memorialized in the Bank's charter and continues to have normative significance with respect to the institution's approach to what is "political."

Although state power is reified through the Bank's board, it is simultaneously diluted as part of the depoliticizing mission. When implementing development projects, Bank officials present state governments as administrative tools for providing services and facilitating economic growth, rather than as agents of political power. Because the Bank aims to bring "development" into a country by means of a neutral state apparatus, "representations which ignore the political character of the state and the bureaucracy and downplay political conflicts within the nation-state are the most useful" (Ferguson 1990, 72). By treating poverty reduction as a technical problem, the Bank can perform "extremely sensitive political operations involving the entrenchment and expansion of institutional state power almost invisibly, under cover of a neutral, technical mission to which no one can object" (256). State politics and the political in general are thus viewed as contrary to the standardized practices and the identity of the Bank.

It is important to note that the official interpretation of the Bank's Articles has evolved over time to reflect incremental expansion of the mandate and a multifaceted view of development, including not only economic dimensions but also political, social, and cultural ones (Darrow 2003). Former general counsel Ibrahim Shihata authored the most influential opinions, which broadened the Bank's scope of work and acknowledged the centrality of human rights within development: "While the Bank is prohibited from being influenced by political considerations, its staff increasingly realize that human needs are not limited to the material 'basic needs' often emphasized in the 1970s. . . . [N]o balanced development can be achieved without the realisation of a minimum degree of all human rights"(Shihata 1991a, 133).

In the past two decades, Shihata's opinions and memos opened legal room for the Bank's involvement in areas that were once deemed too political, such as legal and judicial reform, governance, and anticorruption efforts.

Yet these new agendas had to be depoliticized and instrumentalized in order to gain traction within the institution so as to stay consistent with a seemingly neutral and technical mission. Shihata explained that the good governance agenda he championed "should only be of concern to the . . . Bank as long as it was instrumental in promoting" economic growth (Anders 2005, 45). The Bank has applied the same rationale to its legal and judicial reform projects, which primarily include administrative components (such as providing technical assistance to courts, improving legal education, and training judges) and are focused on private legal reform "as a matter of non-political economic expertise" (Santos 2006, 273). Bank officials have described these projects as reforming governance rather than government because "government [is perceived as] unmistakably political whereas governance de-emphasize[s] the political character and stresse[s] 'management' of administrative and economic resources" (269). Despite the technocratic character of legal and judicial reform projects, their prevalence at the Bank is part of a larger movement among international development agencies to embrace the role of law and institutions.

Legal Globalization

The use of legal instruments as a means of commensuration is a common feature of globalization and neoliberal capitalism, which entails the shrinking of the social, the outsourcing of government, the displacement of politics, the commodification of nearly everything, and the ascendance of the market as hegemonic. It includes but is not limited to a judicialization of politics and a fetishism of the rule of law (John L. Comaroff and Jean Comaroff 2006). John and Jean Comaroff argue that "a 'culture of legality' seems to be infusing the capillaries of everyday life" (25). With the rise of law-oriented nongovernmental organizations and the spread of popular constitutionalism, citizens are appealing to law, and increasingly to the judiciary, to protect their rights. So too are private actors turning to civil proceedings to resolve disputes. As part of the fetishization of law, we see a contractarian conception of human relations and property relations, which facilitates the negotiation of incommensurable values (of relationships, rights, and claims; Comaroff and Comaroff 2000).

In addressing the question of why the legal has been fetishized, the Comaroffs note that legal instruments "appear to offer a ready means of commensuration: a repertoire of more or less standardized terms and practices that permit the negotiation of values, beliefs, ideals, and interests across otherwise-impermeable lines of cleavage" (John L. Comaroff and Jean Comaroff 2006, 32). The resort to legal instruments is part of "law fare," which seeks to impose order by rendering values legible, legal, and legitimate while at the same time displacing the political (30). Lawfare is the vehicle by which the Bank legitimizes its economic and political hegemony. Rather than authorizing itself through ethical claims, the bureaucracy judges itself according to a capacity to meet performance measures and produce results (Rose 1999). The use of legal instruments as a means of commensuration follows from Weber's ideal type of "logically formal rationality," which constitutes the basis of legal domination and economic development for the modern state (1978).

As the resort to lawfare crosses nation-states, we also see a globalization of legal regimes, defined as "the worldwide progression of transnational legal structures and discourses" (Halliday and Osinsky 2006, 447). This phenomenon has reached other development institutions, which have recently pursued legal and judicial reform projects as a way to spread the rule of law. David Trubek and Alvaro Santos observe that, since the mid-1990s, development practitioners have embraced the rule of law as a constitutive part of development itself (2006). The practitioners' interest began in the 1980s, but their vision of law shifted from serving as a framework for market activity to an instrument of state power. In line with recent critiques of neoliberal policies and a purely economic conception of development, agencies began to stress the importance of the rule of law and institutions as part of achieving "good governance." Governance projects narrowly focus on "the effects of governance on growth and aid's impact, rather than a wider concern with equity and justice" (Weaver 2008, 117), thus imbuing law with the logic of economic rationality. Ironically, good governance actually means less government, in favor of nonstate mechanisms of regulation and privatization of state services (Rose 1999). Today, legal reform projects are the business of multilateral agencies such as the World Bank, bilateral agencies such as USAID, and private foundations such as the Ford Foundation (see Carothers 2006). Although there have been many internal and external critiques of such projects and their scant results, developing countries still demand them and agencies have an incentive to continue funding them in order to expand their legitimate sphere of interest, facilitate private investment, and extend their economic hegemony (see Santos 2006).

The phenomenon of legal globalization has also led to the legalization of development institutions themselves and bureaucratization of politics within them. When organizations become more legalized, "law and law-like forms offer a normative source of organizational legitimacy" (Power 2007, 169). In this way, legalization is more managerial than legal; it is about risk management and auditability (2007). David Kennedy notes that development professionals have turned to law "to define development, as the route to development, and most importantly, as the framework and vocabulary for debating about development policy" (Kennedy 2006, 167). This is particularly true within the Bank. To justify their work as falling under the Bank's mandate, employees have attempted to strip law of any political character (however impossible that may be) and treat it as simply instrumental toward achieving economic growth. In doing so, they are consciously appealing to law as an entry point to work on issues that were once deemed too political and thus taboo. We see the effects of legal globalization in a recent legal opinion by the Bank's former general counsel.

The 2006 Legal Opinion on Human Rights

On January 31, 2006, on his last day as general counsel, Roberto Dañino dropped a bomb on the desks of his staff (or, more accurately, into their computers).[9] Members of the Legal Department woke up that morning to an email from Dañino with an attachment entitled "Legal Opinion on Human Rights and the Work of the World Bank." Its topic did not surprise many, since Dañino had championed this issue during his tenure at the Bank and was credited with opening up space inside and outside the institution for a dialogue on human rights. He set up a small working group on human rights only one month after arriving at the Bank. Over the next two years, he strengthened the Bank's relationship to the Office of the UN High Commissioner for Human Rights. He also gave speeches at New York University (March 2004) and the Bank's Legal Forum (December 2005), among other venues, on the importance of human rights to the Bank's work and the need for a more progressive interpretation of the Articles of Agreement.

Soon after Dañino came to the Bank, he began setting the stage for a future human rights opinion. His March 2004 speech at NYU was an early incarnation of the opinion, which he continued to develop over the next year and a half. He had hoped that the opinion would not be an end in itself, but the beginning of a process of mainstreaming human rights from the bottom up and creating a space for more open dialogue. The decision to resign in January 2006 was very sudden, precipitated by a feud with then-President Paul Wolfowitz that resulted in a significant weakening of Dañino's influence within the institution. As a result, Dañino decided that releasing the legal opinion on his final day in office was his last opportunity to bring attention to the issue (despite the fact that he wouldn't be able to follow up) and leave what he hoped would be his legacy in the Bank.

The closing statement of Dañino's legal opinion reads, "The Articles of Agreement permit, and in some cases require, the Bank to recognize the human rights dimensions of its development policies and activities since it is now evident that human rights are an intrinsic part of the Bank's mission" (Dañino 2006, 9). This view represents a significant departure from the previous interpretation of the role of human rights in Bank operations. The last general counsel to issue an opinion was Shihata, who authored the prevailing interpretation of the Articles with respect to considering human rights in Bank operations (see Shihata 2000b). Both Shihata and Dañino interpreted provisions in the Articles that bear on human rights, particularly those that prohibit political activity and permit only economic considerations in decision making.

Dañino's opinion is consistent with a principle expressed by Shihata in his published legal papers: "Rules made to apply for a long period of time have to be flexibly interpreted with due regard to changing circumstances" (Shihata 2000b, xxxix). Although Shihata was the first to acknowledge the relevance of human rights for the Bank, he never went so far as to say (as Dañino did) that sometimes a country's human rights violations *should* be taken into account. He also did not recognize the indivisibility of rights, noting that "there are limits on the possible extent to which the World Bank can become involved with human rights of [a] civil and political nature" (Shihata 1991a, 109). Moreover, Shihata applied a strict definition of *economic factors* as those that have a "'direct and obvious' economic effect relevant to the Bank's work" (Bradlow, 1996, 60).[10]

Dañino called for a "purposive" interpretation of the Articles, "examined against the backdrop of the current international legal regime and the evolving understanding of development" (2006, 3). He explained that it is

> consistent with the Articles that the decision-making processes of the Bank incorporate human rights and any other relevant input which may have an impact on its economic decisions. . . . [T]here are instances in which the Bank may take human rights into account, and others in which it should. Indeed, there are some activities which the Bank cannot properly undertake without considering human rights [5, 7].

Dañino then outlined three increasing levels of Bank involvement in human rights. First, he explained that the Bank *may* take a supportive role by assisting a country in fulfilling its own human rights legal obligations (if it expresses the wish to do so), provided that these commitments "have an economic impact or relevance" (7). Second, if a country has violated or not fulfilled its obligations, the Bank *should* take them "into consideration," again provided that they have an economic impact. So far, Dañino's opinion did not stray very far from the interpretation of Shihata.

In describing the third level, however, involving extreme cases, Dañino differed from Shihata in not requiring any economic impact and stating that the Bank *should* do something: "In egregious situations, where extensive violations of human rights reach pervasive proportions, the Bank should disengage if it can no longer achieve its purposes" (Dañino 2006, 8). This is a major departure from Shihata's view. Yet the opinion did not clarify what Dañino considered to be "extensive violations" or "pervasive proportions." The lack of this further clarification left a danger of ad hoc disengagement based on political factors.

Dañino (2006) highlighted several other significant issues in his opinion: (1) the indivisibility of rights ("the Bank should not make a distinction between different types of human rights," e.g., economic, social, and cultural rights over civil and political rights); (2) the existence of economic evidence that establishes a correlation between human rights and economic growth; (3) a recognition of norms that traverse national boundaries (e.g., "corruption, corporate or financial crimes, money laundering, corruption, environmental hazards, war crimes and crimes against humanity"); and (4) the transformation of the concept of sovereignty in relation to human rights. On the last point, the opinion cited customary international law on human rights and argued that "the balance [between state sovereignty and human rights] has . . . shifted in favor of protecting human rights, with the concept of sovereignty having itself been transformed by the evolution of human rights standards and the pursuit of human rights enforcement at all levels of international law in global, regional and domestic fora" (2006, 7). Despite this statement, Dañino did not go so far as to say that international organizations like the Bank are bound by international human rights law. The only subjects of international human rights legal obligations, according to Dañino, are states.

Finally, the opinion reflected the role of the private sector in influencing developments toward social responsibility at the Bank. Dañino argued that it is "standard practice" among private banks to rely on an analysis not only of economic factors but of *all* factors that affect investments, including social, environmental, and political ones (2006). In his March 2004 speech at NYU that formed the basis of this opinion, he further used the private sector as a model, arguing that the Bank, "although a development institution, is primarily a financial institution. . . . [L]ike its private sector equivalents, [the Bank must consider] . . . the 'investment climate' in the recipient country" (Dañino 2005, 8). Moreover, in an October 2005 speech at the Bank, Dañino compared his experience there with his work on Wall Street, where, he explained, commercial and investment banks are similarly supposed to make decisions based on economic considerations alone. Yet he noted that these banks all maintain political risk units that analyze the political impacts of investments on countries and the political realities of their borrowers. Thus they recognize that political dimensions are relevant factors for decision making (2005).

Dañino's opinion represents a slow progression within the Bank toward greater recognition of the interrelationship between human rights and development. This shift began during Shihata's tenure. Over the past two decades, the line between economics and politics has become further blurred with the inclusion of such issues as good governance and anticorruption in the Bank's operations. Expansion of its work program resulted from pressure exerted by member states and critics (both internal and external) of the Bank's failed structural adjustment lending, as well as a normative shift within economic theory itself (Weaver 2008, 98). Although Shihata's opinions couched good governance reforms as part of the Bank's apolitical ideology, they nonetheless opened the door for a broader governance agenda that continued to expand in scope. By 1998, with strong support from Wolfensohn, "the good governance agenda seemed to have found a 'home' within the Bank's internal bureaucracy, thus setting the stage for mainstreaming the agenda. . . . And once 'on the table,' staff members argue[d], ideas [could] be debated and definitions [could] be broadened" (111–13).

Dañino's strategy in writing this opinion was incrementalism. His audience was not the board (which he felt was not yet ready to move on this issue) but rather senior management and staff, whom he sought to "liberate" by allowing them to finally speak about human rights and gradually advocate for an official human rights policy in the long run. Dañino thus instantiates the ideology of gradualism, a belief that changes occur through small, incremental steps rather than abrupt, revolutionary changes. This ideology is also represented by the institution's "mission creep," that is, a shifting of activities away from the core mandate to gradually incorporate issues once deemed too political. By incrementally expanding the domain backed by the legitimacy of authoritative legal opinions, the Bank has avoided acknowledging that the economic-political division rooted in its founding charter is in fact spurious. Dañino's opinion is ambivalent in this respect. He reiterates some of Shihata's arguments and the political prohibitions outlined in the Articles of Agreement, but he also takes a number of steps beyond existing precedent. Moreover, the style in which Dañino presents his opinion—issued on his last day in office, written without any request from the board, addressed to staff rather than presented for approval to the board (all of which I describe in more detail here)—suggests an ambivalence over the institution's identity and the broader relationship between economy and society.

This moment encapsulates the tension between gradualist liberalism and neoliberalism, and the divergence between the pragmatics of neoliberalization and the theory of neoliberalism, which are constant themes in the cultural history of the Bank (see Harvey 2005). Dañino's opinion reveals tension over the role of the state in development. Under liberalism, the state plays a fundamental role in providing social services such as health care and education. Yet under neoliberalism, responsibility for these services is transferred from the state to the private sector, under the view that the social welfare state had achieved little in maximizing equality and minimizing poverty (Rose 1999). Neoliberalism embraces the market economy through deregulation and divestment of state-owned enterprises. As I shall describe, the Bank's orientation has shifted from social liberalism to neoliberalism to its current approach, which is somewhere in between—making gestures toward a more liberal stance with respect to issues of equity and justice while also reinforcing the still-dominant neoliberal ideology. Critics have argued that since "neoliberalism has been less about stripping back the state than about redirecting it," the Bank's recent reforms are simultaneously "all change but no change" (Bretton Woods Project 1997, 2). I argue that Dañino's opinion should be analyzed in light of the institution's historical trajectory and a shifting of policy paradigms.

Founded to reconstruct Europe after World War II, the Bank until 1961 mainly financed large public infrastructure projects (for instance, power and transportation projects) and invested little in agriculture and social sector activities such as health and education (Rajagopal 2003). The institution was "implicated in the social-liberal desire to make the UN system an apparatus for federalist liberal democratic world government capable of making the post-colonial, nation-building world, through multilateral decision-making and majority vote rule, a welfare society built on the political reason of social-liberalism and the distributed wealth of modern Fordist industrial economies" (Girdwood 2007, 420). With the establishment in 1960 of the International Development Association (IDA, which lends to the least-developed countries) and the inclusion of poverty alleviation in the 1970s as a central objective, the Bank expanded lending to embrace health, education, and agriculture. It began to emphasize the social dimensions of development as well as the role of the state in providing social services.

In the 1980s, the Bank supported a neoliberal approach to development in line with the prevailing political ideology at the time, as represented by the Reagan and Thatcher administrations. With strong support from the United States, structural adjustment loans became widely popular, as did "shock therapy" reform, which seeks to bring about rapid economic liberalization through price and currency controls and privatization of public-owned assets. The Bank no longer endorsed state-led development strategies but instead pushed for deregulation. As a result of a strong public backlash against the social and political costs of structural adjustment, the Bank once again reversed course in the early 1990s. The end of Cold War tensions gave the institution more latitude to target lending toward reforming domestic institutions. It now emphasized "adjustment 'with a human face' and with a much more nuanced approach to the role of government in socioeconomic development" (Weaver 2008, 96), including a return to infrastructure, health, and education.

During the early 1990s, the Bank also embraced the governance and anticorruption agenda as it rearticulated economic theory to emphasize the role of institutions and a legal system conducive to private sector investment. Hence, the positive role of the state became central in creating, monitoring, and enforcing market-friendly institutions (Weaver 2008), thus deviating from the laissez-faire neoliberal ideology. Yet at the same time, the Bank (through Shihata's legal opinions) justified the new governance reforms by defining them as apolitical and driven by economic considerations—thus once again reaffirming the economic-political divide. It is unclear how far the Bank's governance agenda actually departs from the organization's neoliberal ideology. For instance, the Bank's official publications continue to highlight such familiar neoliberal policies as deregulation and privatization, and present good governance as a means of subjecting state institutions to macroeconomic management and constraining states from engaging in excessive regulation and encroaching upon private property rights (Weaver 2008). According to a staff lawyer, legal and judicial reform projects continue to be framed in a mechanistic, apolitical fashion rather than being designed to address the political economy of governance and recognizing that legal institutions are historically and culturally derived:

> Well, the legal and judicial reform movement has been a very sectorized thing. It's been, "Let's look at the justice sector as if it exists as a sector." It doesn't look at the socially embedded nature of legal systems. It just kind of imports them as a structural technocratic thing. So basically if you have an independent judiciary and a law school and a bar association and a court and case management, somehow you're going to have a justice system. And it's just ludicrous. It has been a very strong movement and has been mainstreamed in the sense that development organizations around the world are undertaking these projects. . . . But as far as people actually engaging with the nature of law and what it actually means, I don't think so.[11]

Although the governance agenda is "packaged in the guise of a 'post-Washington consensus,' it contains very few critiques of past neoliberal policies" (Weaver 2008, 112).

Dañino's legal opinion reflects this recent era in the history of the Bank, where the institution has been ideologically divided over the relationship between the economic and political spheres and the role of the state in development. Human rights, like governance reform, is still justified according to prevailing economic models and folded into the Bank's dominant neoliberal ideology; Dañino's opinion states that "the decision-making processes of the Bank [can] incorporate human rights and any other relevant input which may have an impact on its economic decisions . . . provided this is done in a non-partisan, non-ideological and neutral manner" (2005, 5–6). Yet the opinion also recognizes that "in egregious situations, where extensive violations of human rights reach pervasive proportions, the Bank should disengage" (8). Here we see hints of a liberal approach to human rights, as issues that can be addressed for intrinsic reasons despite any economic impact. In addition, the opinion relegates the state to a passive role (by declaring that the balance has shifted from state sovereignty to protecting such norms as human rights, which "traverses national boundaries") while also emphasizing that human rights enforcement is ultimately the state's responsibility and that the Bank's role is "one of supportive cooperation" (6–8). The role of the state is simultaneously supported and neglected.

The struggle between neoliberalism and liberalism is not restricted to the Bank. It is a feature we also see in other international economic institutions that are under pressure to incorporate social democratic issues. For instance, Director-General Pascal Lamy of the World Trade Organization declared "the need to 'humanize globalization' by launching a more welfare-oriented 'Geneva Consensus' to counter-balance the perceived neoliberalism of the 'Washington Consensus' in international trade relations" (Kinley 2009, 54).[12] Yet the WTO and other global governance institutions continue to blur any distinction between a market economy and a market society. The slippage within Dañino's opinion and the internal resistance to its widespread circulation that I discuss here suggest that efforts to resocialize market relations and capitalist enterprise are clashing with embedded ideologies and cultural logics.

The Opinion's Uncertain Legal Status

The 2006 legal opinion seemed to clear the way for the Bank's adoption of human rights norms. It removed a major obstacle—legal restrictions in the Articles of Agreement—that board members and employees had long cited as the reason the Bank could not directly engage in human rights. It also raised the status of Legal Department lawyers, who had played a minimal role in earlier initiatives within the Bank but were now in a position to lead internal discussions on a possible human rights strategy. Finally, the opinion had the potential to spark discussion among staff about the role of human rights at the institution, a topic that had been taboo for many years. The opinion's flexible interpretation of the Articles of Agreement could have created an enabling environment for more explicit work on the issue.

So how did Bank staff react to the opinion? The most common response was silence. This is because the great majority of the staff did not receive the opinion on January 31, 2006, when it was released, or on any day thereafter. It was sent only to members of the Legal Department and a selected number of vice presidents and senior officials. Some of the lawyers then forwarded the opinion to their colleagues in other departments, but many among the staff had not read it, let alone knew that it existed even months after its release. The Legal Department made no effort to circulate the document to the rest of the staff; more remarkably, some lawyers obstinately refused to disclose the contents when asked. Inquiring employees were told that it was the exclusive domain of the Legal Department and could not yet be shared with "outsiders," referring not only to the press and NGOs but also to anyone in the Bank outside the department.[13] Nevertheless, those within the department who supported the opinion and were frustrated that it was being stymied by senior officials proceeded to leak it to NGOs, which subsequently posted it on their websites.

Nondisclosure of legal opinions outside the Bank is a matter of precedent. They are supposed to remain internal, although they have been occasionally leaked externally. Under the Bank's disclosure policy, the general counsel may not release legal opinions publicly without the board's approval.[14] The only prior example of such external release was when Shihata's legal opinions and memoranda were published in a book (Shihata 2000b). In this case, Shihata had "sought a special authorization from the Bank's

Executive Directors" (2000b, xli). Yet the Bank's disclosure policy does not prohibit dissemination of opinions to staff members outside the Legal Department.

Why were senior officials in the department blocking the circulation of information across the Bank? The Legal Department's refusal to circulate the opinion likely stems from internal division over human rights as well as a culture of secrecy. It was an effort to assert the power and authority of the Legal Department in relation to the rest of the Bank. The act of policing the secrecy of the opinion endows officials with social power and the capacity to produce order. Moreover, senior officials recognized the radical nature of the opinion and were afraid to champion the cause to a possibly hostile senior management and board. Because Dañino left the day after he released his opinion, there was no one in a leadership position to defend it and spearhead a follow up campaign at the Bank.[15] One official described the opinion to me as "a bomb that was set off."[16] Human rights had been an issue discussed behind closed doors for years; it has constantly perplexed many lawyers who have struggled over and disagreed about how or whether to reconcile the issue with the Bank's restrictive Articles of Agreement. Officials within the Legal Department were very reluctant to air those internal divisions and uncertainties in public and thereby reveal any vulnerabilities.

Another important reason for the opinion's restricted circulation is ambiguity over its legal status and the resulting uncertainty over whether the Legal Department should circulate it as the Bank's "official" interpretation of the Articles. General counsels customarily write legal opinions in response to a request from the board, which then endorses them as official Bank opinions. In the case of Dañino's opinion, senior Bank management, rather than the board, had asked Dañino for guidance on the issue of human rights.

The opinion was not submitted to the board because senior officials knew that members were sharply divided over human rights and would very likely not approve it. As I mentioned earlier, the board conventionally operates by consensus, so any disagreements between countries over human rights would be enough for the Bank not to approve the opinion. Dañino felt it was not the right time to confront the board on this issue: "It [was] impossible. So that's the reason that I didn't want to go to the Board. . . . Because if you go there, [some of the board members might try to] stop us. There's going to be an impasse. So I just didn't want to go there."[17]

Dañino realized that the activities he was pursuing under the radar would likely be prohibited by board members if they were submitted for approval. Moreover, the board's failing to endorse an opinion would amount to public condemnation of internal efforts to push a human rights agenda forward in the Bank. It could even result in a backlash on the part of executive directors who might then become more vigilant in prohibiting any human-rights-related initiative they deemed contrary to the Bank's mandate. Senior officials felt it was best to operate under the radar with regard to controversial issues such as human rights.

With little chance of the opinion being approved by the board in the near future, its legal status remained uncertain. Under Article IX of the Articles of Agreement, the executive directors have the authority to decide questions relating to interpretation of the Articles. Legal opinions from the general counsel are intended only to offer guidance to the board in deciding these questions. Yet there is no precedent on how to treat opinions unapproved by the board and written by a general counsel who has since departed.

Employees who had read the opinion held widely differing views about its status. A senior member of the Legal Department said it should be treated as "an internal matter, part of an iterative process. . . . It [should be] considered as a source of advice for management, but not the board."[18] Some staff members questioned the process by which it was drafted and its legitimacy as an official Bank opinion. According to a senior official in the Sustainable Development Network:

> A legal opinion is given only when the board or management seeks the advice of the general counsel. And I was talking to [a senior counsel in the Legal Department], and he said that we're not sure where we stand because nobody asked for this. [Dañino] just voiced his opinion. If you voice your opinion, it's like a newspaper article. You can write it, but it doesn't carry legal weight. Legal weight is when a judge is sitting in a court and hears the evidence on both sides and then he makes a judgment. So [the senior counsel] was saying that we don't know how we're going to cite this. Is this his personal opinion or is it institutional opinion?[19]

A senior lawyer in the Legal Department reiterated the unclear status of the opinion:

> In this limbo period that we are in [in] my department, it's hard to say whether that's a mandatory document to follow or not. It's not even allowed to be disclosed outside the Bank yet, although that's pretty flimsy. . . . ['l']he Legal Opinion represents a step forward, and we're going to have to see what is going to be absorbed, rejected, or mainstreamed. Or is it simply going to be something in the books, for the future?[20]

Another lawyer's view was that "as long as this is just a legal opinion of the general counsel, [and] it hasn't gone to the board or it hasn't gone any further than that, [lawyers in the department] will stick to the old practice."[21]

Conclusion

The 2006 Legal Opinion on Human Rights encapsulates tension between gradualist liberalism and neoliberalism within the recent cultural history of the Bank, as well as ambivalence over efforts to socialize market relations and the broader relationship between the economic and political spheres. This ambivalence extended not only to the text of the opinion but also to the style in which it was issued: on Dañino's last day in office, and addressed to staff rather than presented for approval to the board. Its restricted circulation within the Bank is also quite revealing. The opinion's uncertain legal status is an important reason for its limited impact, but this is only part of the story. My research points to other underlying reasons members of the Legal Department did not (or even refused to) circulate the opinion. In the following chapter, I discuss the role of bureaucratic obstacles as well as internal conflict within the department over value-laden issues such as human rights.

Chapter 3

Bureaucratic Obstacles

A Clash of Expertise Within the Organizational Culture

T O UNDERSTAND how bureaucratic obstacles have shaped the adoption and diffusion of human rights norms, one must analyze the Bank's organizational culture. An ethnographic description of an organization analyzes contestation over cultural meanings and practices, shifting relations of power, and historical change. Treating organizational culture as "continually emergent, continually negotiated, and continually in play" (Batteau 2001, 726), anthropologists study what is considered "normal" and what is not (Douglas 1966), and how and why certain meanings and discursive forms become authoritative in particular settings and circumstances (Wright 1994) My study of the Bank's organizational culture adopts this approach as I uncover the power dynamics and contestation within the institution, particularly with respect to human rights.

My study of organizational culture stands in contrast to those coming out of the discipline of organizational studies, which is primarily found in business schools. Organizational studies literature treats "culture" as an object that is static and uniform, and can be defined and measured (Schein 1991). Culture is "an objectified tool of management control" (Wright 1994, 4), such that companies can invest in corporate culture as a way of instilling unifying values and practices among employees (Deal and Kennedy 1982). In contrast, anthropologists offer a more interpretive understanding of culture as a political process of constructing and negotiating meanings, which are continuously contested. According to Jean and John Comaroff, culture is "the historically situated field of signifiers, at once material and symbolic, in which occur the dialectics of domination and resistance, the making and breaking of consensus" (Comaroff and Comaroff 1991, 21). The approach I take here adopts this understanding of culture as applied to organizations.

In offering an anthropological understanding of the Bank's organizational culture, I draw from the contemporary work of several scholars. I benefit from recent ethnographies such as that of Caitlin Zaloom, which explores the practical ethics of markets through the culture of traders in the Chicago futures markets. Zaloom's study is particularly useful for studying global financial markets though the lens of the individuals who work to shape them, and analyzing how those individuals are themselves shaped into economic subjects (2006). William Mazzarella's ethnography of the advertising industry in India similarly examines the everyday life of another type of market, the consumer one. His analysis of institutions of contemporary consumer capitalism (e.g., marketing and advertising agencies) and the ambivalence revealed in their contradictory practices inspires my own focus within the Bank (2003). Another noteworthy contemporary study is that of Bruno Latour, who provides a rich ethnography of French administrative law as analyzed through the inner workings of the Conseil d'Etat (2010). My analysis of the movement of human rights norms through the Bank's institutional culture follows Latour's examination of the "passage" of law, whose meaning is enmeshed in mundane bureaucratic practices. It further affirms his argument that "one could consider all law as organization. . . . The organizational content forms a much vaster set than the rules of law [themselves]" (275).

Finally, my study of cultures of expertise benefits from Douglas Holmes and George Marcus's notion of "para-ethnography" as applied to technocratic regimes and globalized institutions (2005). I aim to incorporate the so-called para-ethnographic dimensions of expert practices, "the de facto and self-conscious critical faculty that operates in any expert domain as a way of dealing with contradiction, exception, facts that are fugitive, and that suggest a social realm not in alignment with the representations generated by the application of the reigning statistical mode of analysis" (237). This method is particularly applicable to studying Bank personnel who "must overcome precisely the subversions of the social that they have had a direct hand in creating through their promotion of neoliberal reform" (238). By examining informants' own interpretive and experience-based knowledge practices, one can gain access to internal critical perspectives that can inform a more comprehensive understanding of global governance institutions.

The Ambiguities of Organizational Life

Studying the organizational culture of a bureaucracy entails an investigation of ambiguities, among them slippage between formal institutional representations and actual practice, internal tensions experienced by employees over the values that guide their behavior, and clashes between domains of expertise. In this chapter, I examine such ambiguities in a variety of areas of organizational life: the institutional mission, incentives, operational policies, construction of knowledge, management structure, and expert communities.

An organization has a "mission" when a clearly defined direction and principal goals lie behind its operations. Although the Bank's explicit mission is poverty alleviation, the Bank has multiple implicit mandates, which have developed over time in response to internal and external pressure. In the 1960s, the Bank broadened the scope of activities to include health, education, agriculture, and housing and later introduced policy-based lending, the environment, and gender, followed by such issues as indigenous peoples and legal and judicial reform (Bradlow 1996). This expansion of the Bank's activities has led critics (both internal and external) to accuse the institution of mission creep, or the shifting of activities away from an organization's original mandate (Einhorn 2001).

Within the institution and in the minds of employees themselves, the core mission of the Bank and the activities that can be considered consistent with it have been continuously debated. Employees often hold perspectives on the basis of their disciplinary backgrounds, although there are exceptions. For example, many of the personnel in the Social Development Department, who are often sociologists and anthropologists, not only view human rights as part of the Bank's mandate but advocate for a rights-based approach to development.[1] Within the Legal Department, some lawyers share this view, while others acknowledge feeling internally divided over the issue.

One lawyer to whom I spoke described a dilemma he faced in Swaziland, which has one of the biggest AIDS problems in the world but also one of the most repressive regimes. Should the Bank stop lending to the country because it unfairly locked up five hundred dissidents, even if this meant closing down the AIDS project, which was significantly helping the poor population? He noted that another problematic issue is whether bringing in human rights would create a double standard—punishing borrower countries for human rights violations while not doing so for donor countries. According to the lawyer: "Those are really difficult questions. I mean, it is easier when you are an academic sitting in a university, . . . and it's another thing where you are sitting on a chair and making decisions and facing the reality every day. So how do you deal with the situations?"[2]

Another employee expressed similar frustration at the clash between her moral beliefs and the pragmatic reality of carrying out projects:

> I find it sometimes easier to take the moral high ground and say that this is good because it's good, and we need to respect people, and I'm all for that. But then you're in Ethiopia, and . . . you face this issue of a pro-poor government that has been doing real things to relieve poverty but apparently they can't handle the political space of the opposition. So what do you do? How do you have a dialogue? What arguments can you put on the table? It was not so easy.[3]

In an organization like the Bank, where "the objectives of the institution are a little unclear, the norms are a little unclear, the roles are a little unclear, [and where] there are so many nationalities [and] so many disciplines," there is uncertainty among employees as to what their priorities should be at work.[4]

Since employees are not trained as to how to balance competing priorities, they end up "shoving [them] back somewhere" (though they never disappear).[5] Without guidance from the Bank on how to resolve these dilemmas, some employees have organized their own support groups to openly discuss difficult issues that implicate ethics and values (see the discussion of the Friday Morning Group in the next chapter). Others, perhaps frustrated with the uncertainty of what to do in these instances, try to abandon responsibility for the moral implications of their actions by hiding behind the political prohibition in the Bank's Articles of Agreement and claiming that ethical issues don't appear in Bank policies. Finally, there are a subset of staff members who explicitly embrace social justice as their end goal, beyond any Bank protocol. As one employee put it: "So if I'm going get fired because I'm trying to do something right, then fine, I don't belong here. That's my attitude."[6] Thus there is a range of attitudes among employees, who are largely left alone to determine how they will personally manage ethical dilemmas.

Socialization conditions employees as to the unstated assumptions behind their work and the issues that are taboo, to be neither discussed nor worked on. *Socialization* refers to "a systematic means by which [organizations] bring new members into their culture" (Pascale 1985, 27). It can occur through recruitment procedures, training, informal conversations with peers, and rituals that validate the organizational culture. Norm socialization processes inculcate employees with the generally accepted values and expected behavior in the organization. Managers can also send signals as to what is valued, by spending time on and asking questions about certain issues but not others (1985). Through such mechanisms of organizational control, the power distribution becomes a social fact and is thus institutionalized and perpetuated (Pfeffer 1981).

One mechanism by which socialization occurs is through incentives (both pecuniary and nonpecuniary), which "tell people specifically what is valued and comparatively more important in the particular setting and how, therefore, to allocate attention and effort among competing objectives" (Pfeffer 1997, 111). The Bank's incentive system could be summed up in this statement: "The culture of the Bank is getting a project to the board. . . . You get your intellectual brownie points from your peers in the Bank by saying that 'I have taken a $200 million project to the board in so many months, and so many years.' That's what gives you standing."[7] Though this incentive is not explicitly stated in staff manuals, it becomes part of the common knowledge of employees soon after they join the Bank. The emphasis on lending targets originates in former President Robert McNamara's tenure in the 1970s and reflects the Bank's need to justify its legitimacy and relevance by rapidly disbursing funds to borrower countries.

Several problems with this incentive system were articulated by an employee:

> It's very easy to measure money-out-the-door but hard to assess your contribution to results. How do you know that it was your project that achieved [a particular result]? Also, managers move [to different departments] and there are big lags in things—people think you can change a country in two

years, but you can't. You need to have a very sophisticated system for assessing your contribution to development in your specific area. And that's hard to do, and it's hard to do it in the time period where they can hold you accountable for that.[8]

As this statement emphasizes, there is a lot of movement among staff, with most people from the operational units moving every three to seven years.[9] Since it often takes many years for projects to yield results, promotion is not tied to favorable long-term outcomes. Rather, it is based on the number of projects approved and the size of those projects in terms of money lent—outputs that can be quantified. Moreover, staff movement makes it difficult to hold managers responsible for detrimental effects resulting from their projects. One frequently cannot find a causal relationship between a manager's actions and a project's long-term effects, since many external factors (e.g., the political conditions on the ground) come into play. Once such deleterious effects have been realized, managers have long since left their department and are rarely reprimanded in their current positions. There are also tacit forms of promotion that employees discover through their conversations with colleagues and personal observations of their peers' career trajectories. One employee had been told by a higher-ranked colleague that in order to be promoted "the relationship to the client doesn't matter at all. Or the impact of your projects. What matters is the perception of senior management about your skills and your ability to convey, particularly to the Board and to senior management, a good image of yourself. That's what matters at the Bank."[10]

The short-termism in the Bank's incentive system has been further exacerbated in the age of neoliberalism, which celebrates ephemerality and the short-term contract (Harvey 2005). The market has become an ethical code, and the pursuit of self-interest has become a moral value. In the words of a Bank employee working on budget reform:

> There's an expectation expressed explicitly that says your target is to deliver $22 billion worth of loans, for example. And then a lot of the behavior you drive is the result of putting in place that very precise target. Because you drive behavior that encourages the institution to do whatever it takes to hit the target. The goal is [to] hit the target. It's not [to] do the right thing.[11]

The pressure to extract as much as possible in material results within a short time frame has resulted in such unintended consequences as environmental degradation. This was confirmed by a Bank manager:

> Within the Bank, [we] tend to be much more focused on a short run, even when there are not crises. If there are microeconomic crises and so on, I mean, obviously we're trying to focus on that. But even when things are going relatively well, and you're trying to promote growth and so on, you may be thinking only in terms of five years, and not really thinking . . . enough about the environmental implications as [you are] some of the actions that you may be supporting in order to promote growth, which is important for poverty reduction. But over the long run, you could actually be undermining things. For example, . . . [t]he nonrenewable resources eventually are going to run out.[12]

Rather than being concerned with the long-term environmental and social consequences of their activities, workers are guided by and rewarded for immediate material gains.

There is thus a focus on outcomes, rather than outputs. In "procedural organizations" such as the Bank, how staff members "go about their job is more important than whether doing those jobs produces the desired outcomes" (Wilson 1989, 164). As a result, there is a disincentive for ensuring the performance of projects once money has been disbursed. According to some accounts, employees are promoted if they are "following what the big donors in that region [want . . . regardless] of whether there were bad impacts on the ground."[13] Much emphasis is placed on how well people write and present in public, and less on what they achieve on the ground. Many employees have observed that promotion "doesn't have any kind of relationship with performance, in [one's] operations or with the clients."[14] Employees are not held accountable for the implementation of their projects or their negative evaluation by the Bank's Inspection Panel or Independent Evaluation Group.[15] One person even observed a negative correlation between quality of projects and promotion. In regard to two projects that received negative Inspection Panel evaluations, their managers were nevertheless promoted to be sector leaders (heading thematic departments).

Hence we see how Bank operations reflect an audit culture, "leading to a system of project evaluation in which what is really being evaluated is the procedural efficiency of action in terms of the agency's mission rather than its substantive impact on the lives of human beings" (Gledhill 2004, 341). This form of governmentality has disciplinary effects on its subjects: "audit thus becomes a political technology of the self: a means through which individuals actively and freely regulate their own conduct" (Shore and Wright 2000, 62). In other words, "experts and bureaucrats are subjectified in two ways: as objects of calculations and as relays for calculations" (Rose 1999, 152). Thus the logic of auditability can penetrate not just management practice but also the individuals themselves, including how they conceptualize themselves as professionals and make sense of situations. Do they set targets for themselves and cast themselves as depersonalized units, thus adopting the norms of conduct that the organization is governed by?

In my experience at the Bank, I saw this phenomenon most starkly among social scientists working on social development, who struggled against their own professional norms in order to adapt to the procedural rationality of the Bank. According to one anthropologist:

> It's very hard to be a task manager, and social scientists have not really been trained in terms of doing things in a structured, systematic, and timely manner, and com[ing] up with practical solutions that could then be integrated into the project cycle. We're trained to be critics—social critique, right?— and to identify problems and issues and challenges and complexity on the ground. That's our advantage. And that doesn't get you very far in a project cycle within an organization like the Bank. So we've had to change our way of working. . . . [W]hat we learned, I think, through working with the Bank is that the traditional anthropologist's or social scientist's approach to things in terms of going out there and experiencing the world and coming out with an ethnography or something similar, it doesn't work. It doesn't work time-wise, and it doesn't work because there's no consistency in the way different people work.[16]

Some employees recognize the penetration of the logic of auditability among fellow staff members and criticize their focus on lending targets rather than on project impact: "I remember this guy telling me so proudly that my loan is the biggest loan ever done for education in Africa. I thought, 'Why is this so important?'"[17] Others consciously commoditize themselves as a form of self-regulation, to improve their fit and therefore career prospects within the organization. For instance, in an orientation workshop for new employees working on social development, one of the speakers announced: "We have to be very concrete, implementable, able to come up with clean policy recommendations."[18] The speaker suggested that staff in social development have to sell themselves to the powerful country directors and increase demand for their services.

One final contributor to the Bank's audit culture is the Operations Evaluation Department (OED, which was later renamed the Independent Evaluation Group), which reports directly to the board. The OED staff audit the auditors, so to speak, by evaluating Bank projects, programs, and strategies and recommending ways to improve performance. In the words of Michael Power, they function as "a second order control of the first order control system, [or a] control of control" (Power 1997, 82). A member of the OED stated that the department may be just "criticizing for the sake of criticizing" and is thus more concerned with the system in place to govern quality than with improving the quality of performance.[19] The department's independence is also questionable; a number of employees described to me how particular OED reports had been watered down as a result of management pressure before being publicly disseminated. Despite the lofty mission of the OED and a supposed image as the conscience of the institution, reports are frequently not followed up and recommendations have not significantly changed staff behavior or the overall incentive system.

The Bank's Environmental and Social Policies

The Bank has adopted a set of safeguard policies that are designed to avoid or mitigate any detrimental impacts of Bank activities and ensure that operations are financially, socially, and environmentally sound. Although the Bank has not introduced a safeguard policy on human rights, many of the existing policies address human-rights-related issues. They include cultural property, environmental assessment, forests, indigenous peoples, involuntary resettlement, natural habitats, and safety of dams.[20] The existence of these policies may seem surprising given the Bank's taboo on human rights. Yet the policies reflect the ambivalence within the institution and neoliberal ideology in general over human rights. In its embrace of particular human rights, the Bank is engaging in their regulatory dimension and attempting to vacate their sovereignty dimension, which arguably is inherent in any conception of rights.

Take, for instance, the indigenous peoples policy, which the Bank adopted as a result of intensive external pressure from civil society advocates. The policy's promotion of indigenous rights is mainly focused on economic issues such as land rights and commercial development of cultural resources. Sovereignty-related aspects such as the political right to self-determination are not mentioned; nor are international legal instruments on indigenous rights, such as the International Labor Organization (ILO) Convention No. 169. During the revision of the policy (a process that took more than seven years),[21] a prominent indigenous rights advocate within the Bank was thrown off the revision committee because he favored incorporating more extensive discussion of human rights, including reference to international legal conventions. There was also heated debate over whether the new policy should include a right to "free, prior informed consent" or a less-stringent requirement of "free, prior informed consultation" leading to "broad community support," which was the standard that was eventually adopted.[22] The right to free, prior informed *consent* has been recognized in international law (see Article 30 of the UN Declaration on the Rights of Indigenous Peoples), but the right to free, prior informed *consultation* is not clearly defined and is considered a weaker standard (see MacKay 2002). When I asked a Bank employee on the revision committee about the distinction between the two standards, he stated, "I think a lot of that has to do with how much there's a real recognition of the rights of indigenous communities to have control over their own destinies, from a political sense."[23] Thus the Bank's support for indigenous rights attempts to sidestep their sovereignty dimension, under the presumption that it is beyond the Bank's mandate and instead falls under the jurisdiction of the United Nations.

Throughout debates with NGOs over the indigenous peoples policy, some employees felt internally conflicted over their allegiance to the Bank and their sympathy with indigenous peoples' concerns:

> There were people who were concerned about social issues within the institution who led the work from inside. And . . . some of our colleagues would . . . [call] us names: "You are indigenous peoples' advocates. You are NGOs planted here." At one meeting someone said, "Why are you here? Why don't you go work with the . . . Rainforest [Action] Network? Or for the Bank Information Center?" . . . We had been facing a situation between a rock

and a hard place. We go outside, and we are damned as conservative, highly paid reactionary lawyers. Here in the Bank, we are lobbying for indigenous peoples. We are advocates . . . and activists.[24]

Employees were also divided over how to interpret particular policy provisions. Even though these policies are presented as objective black-and-white norms, they are implemented subjectively, depending on a project manager's interpretation of such requirements as "broad community support" and "consultation."[25]

What is the indirect impact of the Bank's incentive system on policy compliance by employees? Project managers have discretion regarding how to apply safeguard policies and balance them with other goals. Some managers who are sympathetic to human rights and view them as part of the Bank's mandate are more careful in applying the policies in their projects. Yet they still face pragmatic dilemmas when trying to balance competing principles. One employee noted:

> In the day-to-day operations, very often these principles may contradict each other. For example, we want it to be participatory and for people to have a say and be involved, but at the same time we want projects to go very fast, such that the effects are seen. So at some point, two principles, each one of which is valid, may counteract and pose a certain dilemma. This is not an ethical dilemma, but a more pragmatic dilemma. But very often you can get into real ethical dilemmas. Principles, [each one being] very good and important, may in pragmatic application become a little bit intertwined, and [it is] difficult to observe which one you should now follow.[26]

One of the common dilemmas faced by employees is whether to design projects that, even if important for poverty alleviation, will trigger safeguard policies and thus take more time and resources to implement:

> In practice, there is risk aversion, which means that projects that should be implemented do not get implemented because there is a risk of them having resettlement [and thus triggering the Bank's involuntary resettlement policy]. So consequently, roads do not get built because people hear that the resettlement requirements are so onerous that they would rather not do the projects. But these are people who need the roads and these are countries that need the infrastructure. So not doing the infrastructure—not building

the power lines—is not a good solution because it's precisely those villagers who need the power lines and the power. So we need to ask ourselves, who are we benefiting?[27]

The Bank promotes its safeguard policies as indicative of concern for environmental and social goals, but the implicit incentive system suggests that these goals are not primary. In fact, most employees perceive the policies as impediments to lending because they add constraints to tasks and thereby reduce efficiency and opportunities for promotion. As a result, there is divergence between the Bank's articulation of policies and their day-to-day application.

This disjuncture is evident in the implementation of the Bank's previous indigenous peoples policy, Operational Directive (OD) 4.20.[28] This policy was intended for application to all Bank-financed projects identified as affecting indigenous peoples, but the Bank's institutional practices diverged from the written policy, according to a 2003 report by the Bank's Operations Evaluation Department (OED). The report found that only fifty-five of the eighty-nine projects (or about 62 percent) that could have potentially affected indigenous peoples (as determined by the OED's application of the stated policy criteria) actually applied OD 4.20.[29] Of the fifty-five projects that applied the policy, only thirty-two (or 58 percent of the fifty-five) were assessed as having done so in a satisfactory or highly satisfactory way.[30] A primary reason for this underimplementation was the institutional constraints associated with the Bank's incentive system.

Employees have a financial disincentive to apply the indigenous peoples policy (as well as other safeguard policies), which reflects an institutional bias toward time efficiency and effective resource management: they are rewarded for getting the most money out the door and carrying out the largest number of loans. Applying the policy would mean devoting resources to implement culturally compatible measures (such as indigenous peoples development plans based on data gathered from anthropological studies conducted by the Bank) and negotiating with countries that lacked the political will to comply.[31] Some managers, therefore, view application of the indigenous peoples policy as an onerous requirement that stifles their efforts to efficiently process loans. According to a staff survey conducted by the Bank's Operations Evaluation Department, "There is a perception among respondents that task teams do not have adequate resources to implement the OD [4.20]."[32] Among the respondent comments was this statement: "To work in areas with [indigenous peoples] a TTL [task team leader] is forced to prepare long descriptive studies, often of no substantial utility in project design. A TTL thus has an incentive not to involve these areas."[33] An employee that I spoke to confirmed the perverse impact of the indigenous peoples policy, which may discourage projects that could benefit indigenous peoples:

> If you have a clear community that is benefited or impacted by a project, and you know that you need to prepare an IPDP [indigenous peoples development plan] or have public consultations, you end up going to a different place where you don't have those indigenous peoples nearby. And you have your project ready in six months or one year, less time than a project with this kind of people affected.[34]

Thus the incentive to get the most money out the door means that managers may refrain from carrying out projects that will trigger safeguard policies, which may delay the progress of a loan and increase its expense. Preparing indigenous peoples development plans and conducting meaningful consultations with indigenous peoples are two such requirements. Task managers have

> a strong incentive to make the loan "work[,"] . . . partly because their own success depends on effectively managing aid disbursements and partly because punishments imposed by the Bank for failing to meet Bank conditions lack moral legitimacy. The threat not to make subsequent [loan disbursements] available therefore has relatively low credibility, and the Bank learns to accept partial success [Gilbert, Powell, and Vines 1999, F617].

The pressure to lend money was cited in the Bank's 1992 Wapenhans Report, which studied the effectiveness of lending operations.[35] According to this report, the key reason for the Bank's decreasing portfolio quality in 1992 was "pervasive appraisal optimism" and an "approval culture" that motivates staff to give more attention to the quantity of lending than to quality.[36] Policies can thus become ends in themselves, a rationalization process common in bureaucracies organized around rules, routines, and operating procedures (Barnett and Finnemore 1999, 718, 720).

The "Knowledge Bank"

In the mid-1990s, Wolfensohn began to define the institution as a "knowledge bank," focused not only on lending money but also on production and transmission of development-oriented ideas, analysis, and advice to client countries.[37] By doing so, "existing products and services [were] redefined as knowledge assets, or augmented with knowledge of how they are used" (Davenport 1998, x). Accumulation and dissemination of knowledge on development became a complementary goal to promotion of economic growth (Stiglitz 1999). Yet the question remains: What counts as "knowledge" for the Bank, and how are different forms of knowledge valued and devalued? According to Michel Foucault, knowledge is a regime of truth and inextricably linked to power: "The exercise of power perpetually creates knowledge and, conversely, knowledge constantly induces effects of power" (1980, 52). Following Foucault, we must analyze the mechanisms by which knowledge comes into being and is produced in order to study governmentality. The analytics of governmentality are concerned with "what counts as truth, who has the power to define truth, the role of different authorities of truth, and the epistemological, institutional and technical conditions for the production and circulation of truths" (Rose 1999, 30).

Although the Bank claims to embrace itself as "the knowledge bank," in fact it values only certain forms of knowledge consistent with the high-modernist ideology of technocratic rationality that prevails within the institution (see Scott 1998; Harvey 1989). Economics is the most privileged form and serves as the basis for the institution's framing goals and definition of development success. Economics is also the most favored discipline in the Bank's career structure; the Bank's Young Professionals Program (which places talented individuals under thirty in a fast track to senior management positions) is mostly filled with those having an advanced degree in economics or finance and often from elite U.S. and British universities (Weaver 2008, 77). In contrast, other fields, such as anthropology and sociology, that favor contextual knowledge rather than general predictive models are accorded less status, and professionals with that expertise have to constantly market themselves and justify the value of their "knowledge products" (e.g., social analysis and community-driven development, which are carried out by the employees in the Social Development Department). This justification often means their knowledge has to be subject to empirical testing and econometric analysis, and thus strategically translated to fit the authoritative economic paradigms that represent organizational utility. According to several non-economist social scientists I interviewed, issues such as social development are not perceived as valued knowledge but as costs or obstacles inhibiting the Bank's business of lending and challenging its authorized knowledge system and administrative rationality.

The Bank presents this collection of "knowledge," which it has gathered over many years of experience advising borrower countries, as a comparative advantage over other development agencies, commercial banks, and private investors.[38] Its research departments are unparalleled in the field of development; few universities if any have the depth and breadth of practical experience that is housed in the Bank. Yet knowledge is also the source of the Bank's bureaucratic autonomy and domination (Weber 1948). Through the normative power of its ideas about economic development and unique access to sensitive government data, the Bank exerts significant influence over borrower countries as well as other international organizations, aid agencies, and the academic community. Moreover, within the institution itself, the process of producing a certain type of knowledge regulates power relations among employees and constrains their conduct.

How does knowledge circulate within the Bank, and under what conditions is it produced? The Bank's management structure significantly shapes the processes of knowledge production and circulation. The Bank is divided into two major groups: the operations units and the network units. The former are responsible for carrying out development projects on the ground and maintaining relations with member countries. They are divided into six geographic regional units, whose cultures are quite distinct. The operations units are further subdivided into five thematic areas, including sustainable development, human development, and infrastructure.[39] The latter units constitute the research arm of the Bank and offer advisory services to the operations staff in the form of reports and referrals to experts. These units cover the same thematic topics as the operations units but are not subdivided geographically.

Since 1997, the Bank has operated under a matrix organizational structure, with overlapping geographic and functional units and parallel reporting relationships intended to promote knowledge management. Matrix structures, which became fashionable in the late 1970s and early 1980s, feature a diffusion of responsibility along multiple lines of command (Bartlett and Ghoshal 1990). For instance, an employee in operations may be concurrently responsible to bosses in three units: a country management unit (based in the field), at least one network or thematic research unit in the headquarters (e.g., poverty, the public sector, the environment, or infrastructure), and a sector management unit. The sector management unit is where the employee sits in the headquarters, and it corresponds to a particular geographic region and thematic area (e.g., Latin American sustainable development). It is also responsible for the operations employee's performance appraisal and promotion (although it receives comments from the other units as well).

When the Bank holds a staff orientation training session, it devotes a considerable amount of time to the goals, functions, and benefits of "the matrix environment."[40] One of the primary objectives of the matrix is to facilitate knowledge seeking and sharing through collaboration and teamwork among units. Knowledge sharing can enhance the quality of the Bank's assistance. For example, operations employees are expected to maintain strong affiliations with multiple thematic groups, which provide cross-country comparisons and best-practice examples on a particular issue such as developing a transport sector strategy. An advantage of the matrix structure is that "its multiple information channels [allow] the organization to capture and analyze external complexity" (Bartlett and Ghoshal 1990, 139). Such complexity includes interdependent activities and the need to respond quickly and flexibly to changing environments. Integrating geographical and functional groups can promote innovative ideas and cooperation among staff but also has the potential to produce incoherence in practice.

The matrix system has grown unpopular among many employees who question whether it achieves the stated objectives. Material from a staff orientation training session boasts that the matrix structure enables staff to "balance potentially conflicting objectives." This seems to be a grave problem, because employees find it difficult and confusing to report to multiple bosses, particularly when the bosses assign conflicting tasks to them. Management scholars have reiterated this criticism, observing that "the proliferation of channels [in a matrix] created informational logjams, . . . and overlapping responsibilities produced turf battles and a loss of accountability" (Bartlett and Ghoshal 1990, 139). The training session material itself admits to some of the challenges of the matrix—for example, ambiguous roles and reporting relationships, power struggles, a high level of staff stress, and decision-making problems.

Moreover, in the case of the Bank the matrix structure does not necessarily facilitate cooperation among staff in the interest of promoting innovation. A senior official observed that even though the matrix is supposed to create a marketplace of ideas competing for influence, he was "not really sure that it functions as a perfect market, that the best ideas are winning." He lamented the "loss of resources being spent on running that system."[41] Most of the new ideas come from people in the network, since those in operations are too busy designing and running projects.

The network, which represents a community of professionals united by a thematic work program, serves as the source of new knowledge, although country knowledge gathered by operations staff is also highly valued. The network's centrality in the Bank's management structure indicates the importance of experts in this knowledge-based organization. Despite the matrix's objective of collaboration between network and operations units, there is an underlying tension between them. Operations employees often complain that those in the network do not understand the day-to-day responsibilities of managing projects and dealing with country governments, so that their research is not always relevant to operational work.[42] Not surprisingly, the high priority of expert knowledge in the Bank's work program and management structure makes it an important factor in determining status among employees.

A Clash of Expertise

There are more than ten thousand Bank employees, including about seven thousand based in the Washington, DC, headquarters and three thousand in the field offices. This ratio is the result of decentralization efforts during the administration of former President James Wolfensohn (1994–2005), when many headquarters employees were moved to the more than one hundred country field offices. Today, employees come from about 160 countries and include economists, political scientists, lawyers, sociologists, anthropologists, environmentalists, financial analysts, and engineers, among others.

There are about three thousand economists, while the number of non-economist social scientists grew steadily from about 12 in the 1970s and early 1980s to more than 200 in 1998 to as many as 446 in 2002 (Davis 2004, 18; World Bank 2004, 8).[43] At the same time, the number of engineers (once an influential expert group at the Bank) has decreased. Thus, the dominance of staff members with particular expertise has shifted over time.

Staff behavior is shaped by various factors, among them employees' prior experience, political ideology, personality characteristics, and professional or disciplinary background (Wilson 1989). I focus on this last factor because my interviews and observations point to it as one of the strongest sources of identification among the staff, as well as a basis for sharp internal division. Having undergone specialized formal education, employees derive much of their working knowledge and skills from their professional background and are strongly influenced by professional norms. They perceive their disciplinary background as a key factor in determining their status and opportunities for career advancement within the organization. Many employees I spoke to noted the dominant status of economists compared to other professionals: "They're sort of the first-class citizens, and everybody else is a second-class citizen."[44] According to a staff lawyer, "The mainstream way of convincing and persuading people is an economistic way of seeing things. Unfortunately, all the other disciplines, like social development for example, are forced to use that language to make their case."[45] Those employees who are most successful at doing so will have more opportunities to rise within the organization. One employee noted that "there are even people who are labeled as economists who may not have been trained as economists, just because that's the most legitimate discipline."[46]

Professional groups may exhibit competing preferences over goals for the organization, including visions for what development means and how it can be achieved. Composed of multiple, often competing, groups of professionals, the Bank's organizational culture is an "epistemic community," a "network of professionals with recognized expertise and competence in a particular domain and an authoritative claim to policy-relevant knowledge within that domain or issue-area" (Haas 1992, 1, 3; see also Knorr-Cetina 1999). It is useful to study the role and status of professional groups by analyzing them as part of an interdependent system, where jurisdictional boundaries are in dispute (Abbott 1988). They speak distinct languages arising from their disciplinary training, which may impede understanding and collaboration. In an analysis of policy debates over the topic of social capital, a few employees observed: "In DEC [the Development Economics Vice Presidency], and among country economists and country managers, talk revolves around quantification, statistical significance, and formal models. Among operational staff, the grammar is different—it revolves around usability and, among many of the social scientists, around social and political change" (Bebbington et al. 2004, 44).

The expert communities exhibit multiple, often competing, versions of rationality or value spheres, deriving from their varying technical knowledge and administrative expertise (Weber 1978). Power relations between professional communities are apparent in turf wars, where departments try to assert their authority and influence within the larger organization. As Wendy Espeland argues, "authority is relational [in that] the authority of one field can be appreciated only in the context of its relations to other fields, other experts, and other forms of authority" (1997, 1125). Experts struggle over who has authority and jurisdictional control over specific issues, such as indigenous peoples.

Experts also clashed over how to address the rights of indigenous peoples when they are implicated in controversial but potentially profitable development projects. For example, during the late 1980s and early 1990s, an internal conflict arose between the Bank's Energy and Environment Departments over the Mount Apo geothermal plant project in the Philippines (see Royo 1998). The Energy Department primarily included economists and engineers, while the Environment Department included mostly environmentalists, sociologists, and anthropologists. The departments issued conflicting recommendations on whether the Bank should allocate funding for the Mount Apo project from an already approved Bank energy sector loan. Because Mount Apo is one of the richest botanical reserves in Southeast Asia and the ancestral home of six indigenous groups, a Bank loan to construct power plants and support oil exploration at the site raised serious indigenous rights and environmental concerns. The Energy Department expressed support for the geothermal project at Mount Apo; the Environment Department wanted to find an alternative site (1998). NGOs and local community groups capitalized on this internal division as they constructed a transnational alliance with employees in the environment department against the project (1998).

Because of growing internal and external pressure, the Bank concluded in mid-1992 that the project proposal did not adequately take account of local groups or consider the cultural and religious importance of the area to indigenous peoples (Royo 1998). As a result, the Philippine government had to withdraw the request to allocate funding to the project. This example is an exception among internal conflicts over social issues since the non-economist social scientists who deal with indigenous peoples and related issues (such as the environment and resettlement) have historically occupied a subordinated position within the Bank (see Cernea 1996; Fox 2003). The environmentalists and anthropologists held sway in the Mount Apo project because there was concurrent external pressure on the Bank by NGOs that were ready to exploit the internal divisions.[47]

As a relatively new expert community, non-economist social scientists such as anthropologists and sociologists often struggle to reconcile their norms, priorities, and methodologies with those that dominate within the Bank. They sometimes face tensions with economists and mutual skepticism about the other group's definition of development success. Social development practitioners have feared that "their concerns for people's welfare could put them at odds with the goal of rapid economic development" (Davis 2004, 12). Table 3.1 appeared in a 1995 Bank discussion paper (Box 7, reprinted in Davis 2004, 12). This highlights the differences between the two groups' approaches and priorities, which can lead to conflict over how to design and implement projects. One economist (who is unique among Bank

TABLE 3.1 Disciplinary Perspectives Among Bank Staff

Bank Economists	Other Bank Social Scientists
Focus on individuals	Focus on people as members of groups
See individuals responding to economic interests (information, incentives, etc.)	See people responding to a wide range of social factors, including culture, norms, and values
Emphasize inputs and outputs	Emphasize process
Assume an expert or advisory stance	Assume a listening or learning stance
Strengths: technically rigorous, universal, quantitative	Strengths: holistic, contextual, qualitative, and participatory
Weaknesses: too simple, too reductionistic to be tailored to diverse contexts	Weaknesses: too complex, too particularistic to be policy-relevant

economists for his familiarity with social theory) noted many of these differences as he argued for the need to engage sociologists and anthropologists in policy making:

> By the nature of their disciplines, they tend to be against bureaucracies and large organizations and anything that has anything to do with power. So for all these reasons, many good sociologists and anthropologists don't engage with the Bank. And even if they do, they don't engage in ways that at least the people in the Bank would consider constructive. They engage in an Escobarian/Fergusonian way [referring to Arturo Escobar and James Ferguson, prominent anthropologists of development]. That's very interesting and important work, but it doesn't leave you with a "And then what?" kind of answer.[48]

Non-economist social scientists themselves are aware of their marginal position in policy making.

In 2005, the Social Development Department organized a full-day orientation session for approximately forty staff members with the objective of "making themselves relevant." Employees were advised not just to provide project support but also to contribute policy notes. To increase their relevance and legitimacy in the institution, they were advised to be very concrete and operational. The biggest challenge was semantic: they had to bridge the communication gap with economists by measuring results and using indicators. (Interestingly, I did not find a similar training session for economists to speak better the language of sociologists and anthropologists.) Several recent initiatives by the Social Development Network—including Social Development Indicators and a Poverty and Social Impact Analysis (PSIA)—indicate a trend in this direction, although there have been internal disagreements over whether such strategic accommodations undermine anthropologists' professional responsibilities (see Mosse 2004b). As David Mosse observed: "These are the strategies of a professional group that is marginal and vulnerable, whose work is largely externally resourced through Trust Funds rather than from core Bank resources; people who cannot rest from making alliances, building constituencies, creating space or manufacturing products on whose marketing success their careers and survival depend" (83). It is quite clear that, within the

Bank, forms of expert knowledge are valued differently, and economic knowledge ranks the highest.

The Prestige of Economists and the Dominance of Economic Knowledge

The dominant subculture within the organization is that of economists, whose expertise ranks as the most valuable in this evidence-based institution and whose language is the dominant mode of communication and rationality. Based on rigorous models and quantitative analysis, the discipline of economics makes claims to objectivity and universalism. These characteristics are particularly desirable in fostering efficient operations at the Bank, which entail application of universal models to address development problems in any country, regardless of geography, history, or culture. Moreover, economic rationality reinforces the Bank's apolitical image and neoliberal ideology. Before further explaining why economics has become so dominant, I describe the influential position economists hold within the institution.

Economists have influence way beyond their numbers. They fill the majority of senior management positions (although they do not make up the majority of the staff), and their way of thinking prevails within the institution, including how they define development success. Moreover, they generally hold the prestigious country director positions, which bear responsibility for dialogue with country ministers and budget allocation to the sectoral units at the headquarters. Importantly, however, the Bank employs economists of differing persuasions, among them neoclassical and new institutional, who are also placed in contention for authority.

Economists have their own prestigious research group, the Development Economics Vice Presidency (or DEC), which hires top economists and holders of recent doctorates, mostly from U.S. and British universities. No comparable effort is made to recruit top members of other professions as to recruit economists into DEC, and no serious career track exists for non-economists as there does for economists.[49] DEC economists produce high-quality academic papers that influence the Bank's staff, public policy makers in member countries, and the academic community. Since employees in operations rarely have enough time to write academic papers, and those in the network are often not afforded an opportunity to research topics of their own choosing, DEC serves as an important platform for transmitting new ideas across the institution.[50]

The dominance of a single profession may be harmful for the Bank, as one senior economist acknowledged:

> In my view, the limitation of the Bank up to this point is that we've been wedded to one discipline: economics. So fashions and trends and fads in that discipline have affected the fashions and trends and fads of economic development at the Bank. So why shouldn't the fads and fashions of anthropology or political science affect it? Why shouldn't those fads and fashions be debated?[51]

Non-economists often feel obliged to translate their writing and speech into economists' language and to quantify their observations to gain legitimacy for their ideas. Although non-economists lack the theoretical training, many strive to learn "a craft version" of the economics knowledge system (Abbott 1988, 65). What distinguishes the economics professional from the legal, for example, is that one can claim to be an economist without advanced training or licensing, while one cannot claim to be a lawyer without passing the bar exam (Fourcade 2006). Staff members with other backgrounds may even call themselves economists to gain status; I met a public sector specialist with a public policy background who chose the title of political economist for this reason. This form of "workplace assimilation" has discouraged informed debate between disciplinary perspectives and has created a sense of inferiority among some who are not economists (ibid.).

Why are economics and economists dominant within the Bank? As the primary international institution responsible for post–World War II era development, the Bank has served as a mechanism for the diffusion of economic paradigms and ideologies in state governments. It has moved away from a neoclassical economic mandate based on one-dimensional measures such as GDP growth, but the approach to development (as part of the Washington Consensus) has nonetheless served as a force of economic globalization. The institution exerts financial leverage on countries by conditioning loans and other financial assistance on market-friendly policies, such as structural adjustment and privatization of state-owned enterprises and social services. It also exerts ideological leverage by offering policy advice and presenting itself as a repository of development research and economic expertise; in fact, it serves as the world's largest development research institution (Gilbert et al. 1999). The Bank's influence is part of a broader institutionalization of economics, which is characterized by such factors as "the establishment of a broadly universalistic rhetoric within economic science [and] the transformation of economic knowledge into a technology of political and bureaucratic power" (Fourcade 2006, 156). As a governance institution, the Bank exercises power by producing and managing knowledge. Yet it favors a specific kind of knowledge, one based on economics, which is treated as authoritative above all other types of knowledge.

Yet what is it about economics as a knowledge system and economists as a profession that makes them dominant in terms of prestige and power? What is it about economics as an ideology that has led to its globalization and given it such authority within bureaucracies and in policy discussions in the twentieth century?

The power of a profession's knowledge system relates to its "abstracting ability to define old problems in new ways" (Abbott 1988, 30). Lawyers use abstraction when they write laws; economists abstract using numbers, which they present as objective and thus authoritative. Numbers construct new categories and new relations among people and things through standardization and commensurability and, in the process, "profoundly transform what we choose to do, who we try to be, and what we think of ourselves" (Hacking 1990, 3). As Georg Simmel demonstrates in his analysis of money (1978), commensuration fosters detachment by objectifying subjective values, standardizing relations between often disparate characteristics, and enabling a depersonalization that is critical for bureaucratic and economic rationality. Numbers thereby serve as a technology of distance (Porter 1995), whose authority comes from "their capacity to create and overcome distance, both physical and social" (Espeland 1997, 1107). Social quantification abstracts away the individual and the local, while also creating a universal language that transcends distance (Porter 1995). Porter argues that "reliance on numbers and quantitative manipulation minimizes the need for intimate knowledge and personal trust" (ix). Yet numbers may also serve as a fetish and an object of suspicion; for instance, statistics may be distrusted as a measure of social order, which then creates a demand for more rigorous and uncorrupted statistics (Jean Comaroff and John L. Comaroff 2006).

Numbers display governmentality because they serve as a technology of power that constitutes populations and makes individuals calculable and therefore governable—by others and by themselves. Statistics establish the classifications by which people come to think of themselves and their choices. The logic of auditability can penetrate the individual by "turn[ing] him or her] into a calculating self endowed with a range of ways of thinking about, calculating about, predicting and judging their own activities and those of others" (Rose 1999, 214). Calculation also enables authorities to "act upon and enroll those distant from them in space and time in the pursuit of social, political or economic objectives without encroaching on their 'freedom' or 'autonomy' " (Miller and Rose 2008, 67–68). Numbers and statistics can create "a promise of control" through the administration of everyday life; they can reassure citizens "against the uncertainties of poverty, crime, unemployment, and more recently environmental and technological risk" (Jasanoff 2004, 33). Yet they can also be deployed to create an image of disorder so as to license imposition of order by force. The Comaroffs argue that "where governance is seriously compromised law enforcement may provide a privileged site for staging efforts . . . to summon the active presence of the state into being, to render it perceptible to the public eye, to produce both rulers and subjects who recognize its legitimacy" (2004, 809). Similarly, the World Bank uses indicators (e.g., the World Development Indicators and the Ease of Doing Business Index in its annual Doing Business Report) to rank and evaluate states according to whether their policies and regulatory environment hinder economic growth, which then legitimates the Bank's role in providing aid and thereby exerting more control over poor countries.

Why have officials and the public at large come to appreciate, and even demand, numbers to explain and solve problems? Theodore Porter (1995) has attempted to explain why quantification methods have achieved such prestige and power in the modern world. Weak experts have imposed economic quantification as a strategy for accommodation in the context of intense disagreement, suspicion, and skepticism (1995). Since the early twentieth century, we see the prevalence of cost-benefit analysis in U.S. government bureaucracies, and within economics since the midtwentieth century. State bureaucrats introduced cost-benefit methods and other accounting technologies to achieve uniformity and public trust, and to dispel the notion that their decisions were arbitrary and biased since they lacked the mandate of a popular election (1995). The notion of statistics as the science of state suggests how accumulation and tabulation of facts (e.g., through censuses, tax returns, and crime figures) transforms reality and the qualitative world into a form that is calculable (i.e., "the taming of chance") and thus susceptible to evaluation and intervention (Miller and Rose 2008; Hacking 1990).

Quantitative expertise has become prevalent within the world of bureaucracies as well as in domestic and international public policy making. Economic knowledge has diffused national bureaucracies in many countries throughout the twentieth century (see Fourcade 2006). Marion Fourcade argues that "economics has become central to the nation, then, because the nation has become more economic" (2006, 167). The globalization of economics and the economics profession is related to global circulation of capital (e.g., through public aid and foreign direct investment) and the resulting economic interdependence of nations (2006). The globalization of the law has also created opportunities for economists to enter legal arenas worldwide (Dezalay and Garth 2002). Other reasons for the transnational expansion of economics are the absence of such barriers as national regulations and licensing systems, and the global mobility of students and professors in the discipline (Fourcade 2006). As Fourcade demonstrates, there has been a "transformation of economic knowledge into a technology of political and bureaucratic power," including global diffusion of the neoclassical paradigm for economies, independent of local or historical context (2006).

The World Bank has facilitated the global expansion of capital and the diffusion of economic paradigms, not only within borrower countries but also within the bureaucracy itself. The dominance of Bank economists has prompted the adoption of quantitative methods for social issues and those that may have been politically contested. Some lawyers have turned to quantification to appeal to economists as they attempt to mainstream the issue of human rights.

The Status of Lawyers and the Culture of the Legal Department

Lawyers have not typically served as the intellectual leaders among the staff or key players in policy making and agenda setting, with the occasional exception of general counsels. The great majority of lawyers at the Bank serve in the Legal Department, which is dominated by transactional specialists who work on loan agreements and advise the staff on operational policies and law-related issues (Norton 2001). Aside from a small number in operations who work on legal and judicial reform and other public sector projects, lawyers typically do not serve as project team leaders, and their participation in projects is usually limited to technical legal tasks. Unlike economists, lawyers are not encouraged to spend their time writing academic papers. Although the Legal Department has organized seminars in order to foster intellectual dialogue on legal topics (for example, a two-day Legal Forum in December 2005 and a seminar series with external academics), lawyers are mainly expected to be skilled in a practitioner-based knowledge.[52]

A senior lawyer who had recently been hired as a consultant in the Legal Department was struck by lawyers' lack of prestige in the Bank and the absence of academically minded legal thinkers:

> This place does not necessarily attract the most creative, energetic lawyers. There are many good lawyers here, but many of the people driving legal development are not here. And I don't think this place has the same attraction for lawyers as it does for economists. . . . One could also think about how one could strengthen the legal environment here. One way is to give it a more prominent place in the thinking of the institution. It's very often seen as a support service. But for human rights law and other issues, it would be worth bringing lawyers more to the core. . . . You should also have more lawyers in the operations.[53]

Another staff lawyer affirmed this view:

> It's almost that the lawyers we get in the Legal Department are accidentally good when they're good. We're not getting the top [in the field] and there are no intellectuals. . . . [Y]ou're not really attracting the best minds because if you come here for a few years, it would be very hard to publish at the level so that you can get back into a university. So I think what that means is that there is not an intellectual leadership in those areas. It's not that these people are not excellent practitioners. There's just not that intellectual backing [as there is for economists, who have DEC, the Development Economics Vice Presidency].[54]

The lawyer who made the second statement further noted that, given the dominance of economists, he felt a need constantly to justify the importance of law and its institutions. To gain recognition from social scientists, he had to appeal to hard data that would measure the law's impact. A senior economist agreed, stating that most lawyers in the Bank are bureaucratic lawyers who shouldn't be telling the world how to change their legal systems. According to his experience, "lawyers are usually not social scientists, [so] more lawyers ought to be trained in social science or need to be collaborating with social scientists."[55]

The reputation of the Bank's Legal Department has historically stood at a higher level and shifted over time, often in line with the strength of leadership by the general counsel.[56] The appointment and dismissal of the general counsel is the responsibility of the Bank's president.[57] The role of the general counsel "may vary according to the organization, the time period, and even the personalities involved" (Holder 1997, 207).[58] Whenever the Bank's general counsel has played an influential role in the institution, lawyers in the Legal Department were given an opportunity to go beyond the traditional duties just listed and at times served as policy makers, innovators, and institution builders (Edwards 2008). For example, during Shihata's tenure the Legal Department played a key role in designing the Inspection Panel (ibid.) and launching both the Multilateral Investment Guarantee Agency and the Global Environment Facility (Shihata 1997). In addition, Shihata's legal opinions on governance and the rule of law paved the way for introducing legal and judicial reform projects on the Bank's agenda (Rigo 1997). Yet the general counsels after Shihata, as well as the Legal Departments that they supervised, have been relegated to a weaker position in Bank policy making and institution building. Moreover, since Shihata's departure, there has been a high turnover of general counsels, all of whom have served less than five years compared to Shihata's fifteen. The Legal Department's ever weaker leadership in Bank decision making following the Shihata period has made it difficult for lawyers to assert substantial influence on the issue of human rights.

Perhaps because of their lower status and their desire to preserve jurisdictional control over legal issues, lawyers—and those in the Legal Department in particular—exhibit a culture of secrecy. This feature is evident in their response to the 2006 Legal Opinion on Human Rights, including its limited distribution and their reluctance to talk about it openly, as well as in their everyday practices. The act of managing the circulation of information and controlling what lies in the public domain endows members of the department with a social power within the economist-dominated institution. They have exclusive control over the interpretation of opinions and internal legal notes, which is expected given that they hold specialized expertise in this area. Yet it may seem surprising that they also have exclusive *access* to the opinions and legal notes, even when the materials directly relate to the work of employees outside the Legal Department. If a Bank employee who is not in the department entered the department's intranet site, she would have access to all documents except the section on legal opinions. She would be immediately prompted to provide a password, which is given only to members of the department. This has not always been the case. Legal opinions used to be accessible to all Bank staff, but the practice ended once lawyers felt challenged by nonlawyers in operations, who had criticized some of their legal interpretations.[59] Moreover, there is a special law library of the Bank that permits only limited access to Bank employees who are not in the Legal Department.

Access to opinions and the law library is even restricted to the small number of lawyers who work in units outside of the Legal Department. I spoke to a lawyer in operations who had been writing a working paper on a human-rights-related topic that required citation of Shihata's legal opinions. When he attempted to gain access to the opinions at the law library, the librarian refused to show him the opinions because he was not a member of the Legal Department (even though he was a lawyer). After becoming suspicious of why someone outside the Legal Department would request access to the opinions, the librarian called a senior counsel in the Legal Department to follow up on the employee. The senior counsel informed the lawyer's boss in operations that the lawyer should not be writing on this topic, since interpretation of the legal opinions is the exclusive work of the Legal Department. The senior counsel did not want anyone outside the department—even a lawyer—to challenge the department's interpretive authority.

As is the case for any department or organization, there is internal conflict within the Legal Department. There are those lawyers who favor a conservative, formalistic interpretation of legal issues, while others adhere to a progressive one. For example, the 2006 legal opinion did not represent a unity of views within the department over the Articles of Agreement. It was drafted by a group of five lawyers led by Dañino and was circulated within the department for comment. Although there was a general convergence of views and no strong opposition, some lawyers preferred a more cautious approach and later questioned its status as an official legal opinion.

Even after the opinion was released, within the department there surfaced resistance to openly discussing and publicizing it. An informal group of lawyers approached one of their superiors about how to foster open dialogue inside the department on the opinion's practical implications. The lawyers considered this an opportune time to spark an internal conversation about the role of human rights, which they considered long overdue. Yet they knew that proposing a Bank-wide discussion would have been too radical at that moment, since it might have appeared to challenge the authority of the Legal Department. Instead, they suggested a safer alternative: a brown-bag lunch that would be restricted to members of the department. (Brown-bag lunches are low-key events, as opposed to daylong seminars or conferences.) Nonetheless, the senior official in question rejected such an event because he viewed the subject as "too controversial."[60] This resistance demonstrates a cautious attitude among members of the department and unwillingness on the part of some lawyers to promote discussion of new ideas. Thus internal conflict inhibited the Legal Department from presenting a united position on human rights and from leading staff in an open discussion in light of the recent opinion.

Conclusion

One cannot analyze the diffusion of norms within an institution without understanding its organizational culture, including norm socialization processes, the incentive system, power dynamics among professional groups, and internal contestations within departments. The World Bank's organizational life exhibits a variety of ambiguities: slippage between the institution's official mission and multiple implicit mandates, clashes between domains of expertise, and ethical dilemmas among employees as they balance competing values and priorities. Its incentive system, which is largely based on lending targets and favors short-term results rather than long-term impact, has resulted in underimplementation of the Bank's social and environmental policies. The logic of auditability penetrates not only the system of project evaluation but also the staff members themselves, who struggle to adapt to the procedural rationality of the Bank.

The culture of the Bank is perhaps most apparent in how it values different forms of knowledge and thus how it effects power. Economic knowledge is the most privileged form, as reflected in the institution's definition of development success as well as the status given to various expert communities and their respective value spheres. The dominance of economists and the lower status of lawyers shape how human rights have entered the institution. Though the 2006 legal opinion had the potential to usher in a new approach to human rights, internal conflict and a culture of secrecy within the Legal Department contributed to the opinion's limited impact. Although the opinion remained in legal limbo with no champion to promote it, a small group of lawyers persevered in their quest to push the human rights agenda forward through other means. In the next chapter, I describe the efforts of these lawyers to frame human rights to appeal to the economist-dominated organizational culture.

Chapter 4

Reconciling Interpretive Gaps

Economizing Human Rights

H OW DOES THE CLASH OF EXPERTISE within the Bank's organizational culture shape the internalization of human rights norms? To bring about internalization, actors must "vernacularize" norms, or adapt them to local meanings and existing cultural values and practices (Merry 2005, 2006b). In this chapter, I focus on "interpretive gaps" as a critical obstacle to operationalizing human rights and achieving widespread norm internalization in the Bank. I analyze how professional subcultures within the organization correspond to distinct interpretive frames on human rights (see Barnett and Finnemore 1999). Interpretive gaps refer to the differences between employees' interpretations of human rights, including how they define human rights, justify their relevance with respect to the Bank's mission, and conceptualize their practical role in Bank operations. Of course, interpretive gaps are only one obstacle to achieving norm internalization. Other factors include lack of an appropriate staff incentive system to motivate behavior, little leadership by senior and middle management, and insufficient investment of resources to effectively institute policy changes. But I argue that in the case of the Bank, the clash between an intrinsic interpretive frame and an instrumental one is an underemphasized factor that has hindered the development of a human rights consciousness among staff. It reveals contradictions within the Bank's bureaucratic culture, which exhibits a tension between principles and pragmatism. Before analyzing the competing interpretive frames, I first review the evolution of human rights as a taboo in the institution.

Evolution of the Human Rights Taboo

The issue of human rights has been and continues to be a taboo at the institution, but the type and extent of the taboo has changed over time and in different contexts. Human rights norms are not systematically incorporated into staff decision making or consistently taken into consideration in projects (although there are minor exceptions that I discuss here). Not only have human rights not been incorporated into the Bank's official policies, they are also not openly discussed within many parts of the institution. Many employees consider it taboo to discuss the topic in everyday conversation and to include references to it in their project documents. The Bank is an environment of tabooed topics, which become part of the everyday consciousness of employees and are encoded in their daily routines. Employees have been socialized to adopt a set of attitudes and beliefs about the human rights of their work and the role of human rights in the Bank in general. Even though staff members clearly face moral or ethical dilemmas in their work, they are usually not encouraged to discuss them publicly.

In my interviews with employees from a number of departments, I found repeated references to the taboo of mentioning human rights. Here are a couple of excerpts:

> The Bank is very skittish about using the words "human rights" because in some countries [especially Middle Eastern countries and China], that's a dirty word that means American or Western values. . . . [Employees] have come to the conclusion that you can't call it "human rights," but you can call it a lot of other things . . . like empowerment.[1]

> There's a real case for human rights literacy at the Bank and demystification. But that alone is not enough. The way we've had it up until now is that we didn't discuss it; staff didn't know about it, [and] staff couldn't possibly have had an interest in it. There was just an assumption that human rights was something that lay beyond the mandate of the Bank. . . . You can't have a groundswell of support without some consciousness raising with respect to human rights.[2]

Employees who were human-rights-literate met resistance in their attempts to promote the agenda. A young staff member suggested at a Bank conference that employees should hand out material to raise staff consciousness about human rights issues. She said that a senior official admonished her and told her that it was not the staff's role to serve as advocates.[3]

The taboo against talking about human rights is part of a larger taboo against explicitly addressing ethical issues in general. According to a senior official, much of the Bank's work revolves around an ethos of technical excellence and objectivity. Employees are discouraged from discussing rights and wrongs, and instead encouraged to talk about trade-offs. When this official met with staff about ethical issues, she found that "people [felt] that they are expected to do things or asked to do things in countries which they're not necessarily comfortable with."[4] She further mentioned that the Bank's institutional culture with regard to ethics contrasts with that of the Office of the UN High Commissioner for Refugees, where she had briefly worked. At the UNHCR, ethical and moral issues were constantly on the agenda and discussed openly among staff.[5] The Bank's taboo on discussing ethics makes it comparable less to a UN agency and more to a scientific bureaucracy, dominated by professionals with technical skills who value measurable, objective data as evidence. For example, among nuclear scientists at Los Alamos National Laboratory in New Mexico, "the ethical dimensions of their own work was [sic] never a topic of conversation" (Rosenthal 1990, 123; see also Masco 2006). The same was true for the Lawrence Livermore National Laboratory in California (Gusterson 1996).

The strongest enforcers of the taboo have historically been lawyers in the Legal Department. Since the lawyers are responsible for interpreting and applying the Articles of Agreement, they are the most cautious in including references to human rights in project documents. In 2004, when the Social Development Department wrote its strategy paper, the Legal Department required deletion of any references to "human rights." The authors of the paper had to resort to using less political words such as *inclusion, cohesion,* and *accountability* (World Bank 2005). It is therefore surprising that certain members of the Legal Department have been recently spearheading initiatives on human rights. According to a senior official at the Bank, the Legal Department felt a particular burden to take up the human rights agenda since it had been responsible for policing Bank discourse on the topic for so many years.[6]

Aside from the Legal Department, there is significant self-policing among employees. Here was the experience of one employee who wrote a report discussing the place of justice reform in the Bank's development agenda:

> I mentioned the [phrase] "human dignity." The feedback that I got from one colleague was to say, "Oh 'human dignity'—that sounds like human rights. You can't write that." And I was like, "Excuse me, that's ridiculous." There is this sort of self-censorship that you witness, and I think it would be much better and productive to open that up and address the issues that we deal with anyway. And address them openly.[7]

Self-censorship is a manifestation of the neoliberal governmentality that pervades the Bank, where the logic of auditability penetrates not just organizational practices but employees themselves. As Miller and Rose observe, "In advanced liberal democracies, [technologies of government] increasingly seek to act upon and instrumentalize the self-regulating propensities of individuals in order to ally them with socio-political objectives. . . . Personal autonomy is not the antithesis of political power, but a key term in its exercise" (2008, 51, 54). Bank employees not only are promoting neoliberal dogma in developing countries but are themselves imbued in it through conscious self-control, as exemplified in their self-regulation of the human rights taboo.

As official rhetoric on human rights shifts over time, the taboo has also changed in type and extent. As I describe next, there have been various manifestations of these changes within the institution.

Selective Application of the Taboo (by Topic and Country)

The taboo against working on or speaking about human rights has not applied equally to all rights, sectors, and countries. Historically, the institution has more openly engaged in economic, social, and cultural rights, such as the rights to education and health. Civil and political rights have not been historically recognized as part of the Bank's work since they are interpreted as beyond the Bank's mandate and not directly related to its mission of poverty reduction. Because these types of rights raise sovereignty-related issues, they more directly challenge member states and have been resisted for many years. Despite the Bank's recent encroachment into particular issues such as legal and judicial reform and corruption, it continues to demonstrate a contradictory stance toward civil and political rights, for example, by refusing to fund criminal justice components such as police, prosecutors, and prisons. The inability to include components of this sort has impeded the work of Bank employees in such countries as the Sudan, where support for police and prisons is critical in any development initiative.[8] With the Bank's refusal to fund these so-called political issues, other donors like the UNDP have taken a leadership role in administering criminal justice projects in poor countries.

The Bank has addressed human rights more openly with regard to particular rights holders, including indigenous peoples, as a result of intensive external pressure on behalf of these populations. For instance, its indigenous peoples policy is the only operational policy that explicitly uses the term *human rights*; it aims to ensure that "the development process fully respects the dignity, human rights, economies, and cultures" of indigenous peoples.[9] The Bank does not have a similar policy to address the rights of other vulnerable peoples, such as ethnic minorities, although its projects have targeted distinct minorities including the Roma in Eastern Europe and Afro-descendants in Latin America. In the area of gender equality, the Bank has applied a rights-based approach as delineated in its 2001 report, *Engendering Development: Through Gender Equality in Rights, Resources and Voice.* In addition, Country Policy and Institutional Assessments (a rating system for determining resource allocation to the poorest borrower countries) include ratification of the Convention on the Elimination of All Forms of Discrimination Against Women (CEDAW) as a criterion for consideration in funding decisions.

Moreover, Bank employees selectively apply the human rights taboo for projects in certain countries but not others. For example, they avoid using the term or taking a rights-based approach in powerful countries that have voiced strong opposition, notably China. These countries, which could easily seek funding from the private sector, are important borrowers from the Bank and a significant source of its revenue. Because the Bank cannot afford to lose their business, employees working on projects in these countries are often pressured to avoid explicit references to human rights for fear of angering government officials. In this way, there is an underlying tension within the institution between acting as an investment bank and serving as a development agency.

Some employees who are sympathetic to the rights-based approach have nonetheless avoided it and instead pursued a more incremental strategy when working with very low-income countries:

> In a country like Haiti where the budget is so small, it wouldn't be very help-ful to talk to [Haitian government officials] about a broad human rights ap-proach to everything they need to do. And then this poor government . . . would say, "Oh, what do I do first?" And we'd give them a list of six hundred things, and they'd throw in the towel. And what would we do then? So based on what their budget is and where we think they have capacity and where there's some ownership and communities around it, that's where you move forward first and hopefully produce results that then gives [sic] them a bit more legitimacy and credibility and you push a bit further. . . . So we had to sit down and decide what is the trade-off between focusing on infrastructure and education in Haiti before health.[10]

Determining how to make such a "trade-off" is difficult for many employ-ees, especially those who came into the Bank with idealistic visions of how development works.

Inconsistent application of the human rights taboo—for certain types of rights, in some countries but not others, and for specific populations such as indigenous peoples but not other vulnerable minorities—reveals the Bank's ambivalence over the issue of human rights as well as the political factors that inform how the Bank determines what is "political." Despite the institu-tion's apolitical image, employees are guided by the level of external pres-sure from NGOs and the influence of particularly powerful member states, which result in blatantly political decisions over whether and how to apply the human rights taboo.

Explicit Exceptions to the Taboo

There are settings in the Bank where the human rights taboo does not ap-ply at all. Internal critics have made space within the institution where they can discuss controversial topics such as human rights and forge alliances with external advocates. The most prominent example is the Friday Morn-ing Group (FMG), also known as the Values in Development group, which serves as a tolerant venue—an "oasis" in the words of one member—for the exchange of new ideas.[11] The group began in 1981, when six staff members agreed to meet for six weeks to discuss how their differing religious traditions help them resolve daily ethical dilemmas at work (Marshall and Van Saanen 2007). Since that time, this small group has continued to meet every Friday morning at eight o'clock to candidly discuss the values in the Bank and development work more generally. After a moment of silence that begins each meeting, participants (mostly Bank staff, ranging from secretaries to vice presidents) and outside speakers are asked to talk about the ethical values that motivate their work, and how they relate to the values supported by the Bank (Beckmann et al. 1991). The group is considered "a rare 'safe space,' a place where there is respectful support for ideas and gentle or not so gentle challenges and questions" (Marshall and Van Saanen 2007, 7).

Many issues that were once considered controversial (because of their political undertones) and later became mainstream in the Bank were first introduced at the FMG. Examples of such topics are the environment, corruption, debt relief, and indigenous peoples.[12] Employees have also discussed ethical dilemmas in operations, such as the controversial China Western Poverty Reduction Project in 2004 that led to protests by human rights NGOs on behalf of the people of Tibet. At the time of the incident, the FMG scheduled a discussion between a Bank director from the East Asia region and representatives from the International Campaign for Tibet and two other NGOs. In this respect, the FMG has encouraged an open exchange of views regarding important human rights issues facing staff.

Another alternative outlet that sprang up in 2005 was the Critical Development Thinking (CDT) Group, composed of young Bank employees and external activists who share a commitment to social justice and seek to bring critical perspectives into their work. In addition to organizing discussion and debate on alternative approaches to development, the CDT Group met with former President Paul Wolfowitz and established a regular channel with his office to share recommendations on promoting accountability. To take action on such priority topics as human rights, ethics, and social justice, the CDT Group formed alliances with NGOs (among them the Bank Information Center) and invited speakers from the landless workers movement in Brazil and other social movements. In doing so, members of the CDT Group pursued external venues to bring up human rights and other concerns perceived as taboo within many parts of the institution. The group became largely inactive after its founder left the Bank in 2008.

The presence of these informal bodies has not significantly undermined the overall human rights taboo among staff. Members of the CDT Group were largely young employees and short-term consultants, so they had marginal influence over the general staff. (The FMG does include many senior officials.) Only about twenty to thirty members regularly attend the FMG meetings, although its listserv includes many more. The small attendance is partly due to the time of the meetings; the group meets on Friday mornings at 8:00 A.M., which precludes among others those who are on an alternative work schedule that allows them to take every Friday off. Another reason for the FMG's limited impact on the overall human rights taboo is internal disagreement over the extent to which the group should engage in outreach to other staff and serve in more of an advocacy role. One participant explained:

> If it were up to me, we would do a lot more publicity and put notices out. At this point, it's just word of mouth. You really have to know someone who happens to go to it. . . . There had been times when people said, "Well, shouldn't we take action? Isn't there something we should do?" And the members at the time made a conscious effort that whatever actions you take are your own actions. They couldn't agree then on "Do you support this, or do you act on that?" And then once you start to take action, everyone has a different idea of what kind of action should be taken. So they decided consciously for it not to be an action-oriented group. So you won't see a group from the Values in Development group [FMG] get together and help support something.[13]

But even though the FMG hasn't taken an activist stance in support of human rights, its existence indicates that cultures of resistance are challenging the human rights taboo in the Bank.

Variations of the Taboo

While there is a taboo among many employees as to explicitly invoking human rights, the taboo has not extended to *implicit* human rights work. Some Bank officials who are committed to human rights principles still frame their work in alternative terms. Scholars have called this practice "rhetorical repackaging" (Uvin 2004). In addition, some employees adhere to a capability approach,[14] which shares many of the same concerns as the human rights approach, notably the importance of human freedom and dignity.

To capture some of the meanings behind human rights without using the term, Bank employees have referred to other principles such as social development, participation, inclusion, social accountability, transparency, good governance, and empowerment. These terms are considered "bywords" that, as one employee explained, are simply "different filters on the same lens."[15] Employees prefer them to rights language because they are considered less political, more easily defined, more receptive to measurement, and more negotiable to trade-offs. As a result, "you avoid all the internal obstacles as well as [the] board's obstacles, and you could still do the same job."[16] Yet at the same time, the words do not carry the legal and rhetorical weight that *human rights* does. One Bank lawyer expressed misgivings about "how much violence you do to the concept of human rights by going very far under other banners and other discourses." He was frustrated over "the lack of recognition [among Bank staff] of the limits of doing human rights work but calling it something else."[17] Thus one way the taboo has changed in recent years is that employees are adhering to human rights principles but framing them in alternative terms. The question remains whether such framing dilutes the substance of human rights.

Another variation on the taboo is that employees are supporting certain interpretations of human rights while avoiding others. The recent human rights initiative spearheaded by members of the Legal Department reveals a preference for an instrumental interpretation of human rights over an intrinsic interpretation. These competing interpretive frames roughly correspond to competing expert communities within the Bank.

Competing Interpretive Frames

The distinct interpretive frames held by professional subcultures within the Bank shape their understanding of issues and their preferred strategies for implementation (see Howard-Grenville 2006). Members of subcultures "share a set of problems commonly defined to be the problems of all, and routinely take actions on the basis of collective understandings to the group" (Van Maanen and Barley 1985, 38). Their distinctive worldviews and normative commitments often derive from their professional backgrounds, as with law or economics. A Bank lawyer discussed how disciplinary background shapes the way in which employees frame and interpret the issue of human rights:

> [With regard to] the two disciplines [of law and economics, there is] a very normative approach to the human rights agenda and a too technocratic approach on the development side. The human rights agenda is dominated by lawyers, and the development agenda is dominated by development specialists, mainly economists. And their way of thinking is totally different. Their training is different, their thinking is different, their tools are different. They might come to the same conclusions or they might share the same opinion of the usefulness of a project, for example, or the soundness of a project. But very often this cross-disciplinary discussion is not fruitful, simply because when I discuss with an economist, for example—and that is something we face every day in this institution, of course—I don't have that economic background and I find it sometimes difficult to judge whether what the other person tells me should be convincing for me or not. Simply because I cannot judge the soundness of his argument because I don't operate in the same scientific set of tools. To me, other arguments may be more convincing because I'm used to that kind of argumentation, in a more legal discourse.[18]

Because economic language is the dominant way of persuading people, staff feel that employing it "raises the bar" for arguments based on other disciplines to be accepted.[19]

The two main interpretive rationales for understanding the value of human rights for the Bank and development in general are the intrinsic and instrumental frames. They correspond roughly to distinct disciplinary ways of thinking, although they are not restricted to professionals of each discipline. In my comparison of staff interpretations, I exclude employees who completely oppose the integration of human rights into the Bank's work. This group includes employees from a variety of disciplines who oppose human rights for multiple reasons (including their view that human rights is a political issue prohibited under the Articles of Agreement, opposition by members of the Board of Executive Directors, the lack of expertise within the institution on this issue, a view that human rights falls more within the mandate of other international organizations such as the UN, and a fear that the Bank would condition lending on human rights compliance). In my typology, I focus on those employees who are willing to consider the incorporation of human rights in the Bank, although they disagree on what such an incorporation would look like because of their divergent intellectual orientations.

Intrinsic Frame

Proponents of the intrinsic frame view human rights as universal and indivisible, and they value protection of human rights as an end in itself. There are two subgroups within the intrinsic frame; the first emphasizes the legal dimension of human rights, while the second emphasizes their moral dimension. Those within the first subgroup define human rights as legal obligations deriving their legitimacy from the international human rights regime, and in particular the Universal Declaration on Human Rights.[20] Members of this subgroup include, not surprisingly, many Bank lawyers, as well as civil society advocates who are accustomed to making legal arguments in their campaigns. They view rights as implicitly conferring legal duties on state governments. The Bank lawyers who are committed to this interpretation have expressed grave concerns about any attempt to dilute the basic legal tenets of human rights and to water down the corresponding obligations.[21]

Members of the second subgroup of the intrinsic frame define rights as primarily ethical principles or moral imperatives, founded on a conception of fundamental human dignity and a framework of common values. They often advocate for a principles-based approach focusing on ethics and social policy goals that are not necessarily attached to legal standards. Members of this subgroup include many non-economist social scientists, such as anthropologists and sociologists, who are committed to human rights principles but not wedded to a legal framework. They think this "commonsense approach" of avoiding a formal legalistic interpretation accords them greater flexibility and a better chance of convincing the Bank's skeptical economists, and possibly its Board of Executive Directors, to support a human rights approach.[22]

One manifestation of this interpretive frame is the Bank's report *Principles and Good Practice in Social Policy,* which was primarily drafted by employees in the Social Development Department (World Bank 1999). Rather than recommending that the Bank assist its member countries in realizing their international human rights obligations, the paper advises the Bank to "distill . . . lessons of good practice to assist its members to draw upon them in support of their economic and social development goals" (1999, 2). It lists a set of "generally agreed principles," while noting trade-offs that may arise in achieving them. Under an overarching goal of "the promotion of social development of all the world's peoples,"[23] the principles fall within four areas: achieving universal access to basic social services; enabling all men and women to attain secure, sustainable livelihoods and decent working conditions; promoting systems of social protection; and fostering social integration. Another application of the moral intrinsic frame is the Bank's Social Development Strategy (2005), which is based on the three operational principles of nondiscrimination, inclusion, and accountability. In some respects, the moral frame attempts to bridge the instrumental and intrinsic interpretations by recognizing the universality of human rights principles as well as the need for member countries to translate those principles into practical country-specific results.

Instrumental Frame

Adherents of the instrumental frame provide a functionalist rationale for promoting human rights as a means to an end (which, in the Bank, is economic growth). They value human rights according to whether they enhance development effectiveness and make good economic sense. Given their pragmatic orientation, proponents of this approach often mention trade-offs that employees may need to make when implementing human rights, especially in countries with limited resources. They prioritize the fulfillment of rights that achieve poverty reduction and economic growth. Because many economists typically adhere to this interpretive frame, it carries a lot of weight in the institution.

The Bank's private sector arm, the International Finance Corporation (IFC), adopted this approach to human rights in its recently revised performance standards.[24] In coordination with the International Business Leaders Forum and the UN Global Compact, the IFC also developed a human rights impact assessment tool so that corporations can identify and address human rights challenges in projects on the basis of a model of risk management. As a justification for this work, the IFC made a business case for incorporating human rights by arguing that doing so safeguards reputation and brand image, helps companies gain a competitive advantage, improves recruitment and staff loyalty, fosters greater productivity, ensures active stakeholder engagement, and meets investor expectation (International Business Leaders Forum et al. 2010). The concluding chapter elaborates on how the approaches to human rights differ between the World Bank and IFC.

Table 4.1 summarizes the differences between the instrumental and intrinsic frames·

TABLE 4.1 Human Rights Frames

	Rationale	Conceptual Foundation	Dominating Discipline
Instrumental frame	Functionalist	Differentiated rights according to a growth-based understanding of development	Economics
Intrinsic frame		Universal principles based on:	
	1. Legal	the international human rights regime	Law
	2. Moral	human dignity and ethical standards	Sociology/Anthropology

Operational Implications

How do the competing human rights frames translate into practical effects in Bank projects? I contend that there are operational implications for how employees, particularly Bank lawyers and economists, interpret human rights. For instance, during discussion of a justice reform project, lawyers and economists in the project team disagreed over whether to fund criminal justice components. A justice reform project typically includes funding only for the training of judges and administrative support for courts. Many economists have interpreted criminal justice issues as too political, but some lawyers maintain they are necessary to effectively maintain the rule of law.

A lawyer who supported the inclusion of criminal justice components admitted he had faced problems convincing some economists on his project team that crime and violence are in fact development issues. The lawyer considered the issues important because they may lead to severe human rights violations. But the only way he could convince economists of their relevance was by presenting quantitative evidence that crime and violence increase the costs of doing business, for instance by lowering investment and employment growth, and in that way impede economic growth. However, even after the lawyer attempted to quantify the benefits of the criminal justice components, the economists argued that they were too costly to include in the project given its limited budget. The refusal to include the components frustrated the lawyer, who felt there are certain issues, like those related to human rights, that should not be subjected to cost-benefit analysis.

This example illustrates how interpretive gaps between lawyers and economists have posed an obstacle to implementation of certain human-rights-related issues in Bank projects. What we are seeing here is a clash over the commensuration of values such as human rights. Commensuration, which allows comparison between different qualities according to a common metric, is a feature of bureaucratic rationality and has been crucial for the Bank's operations and the development of capitalism in general (see Espeland and Stevens 1998). The Bank economists described here are seeking commensuration for issues such as crime and violence because it offers a standardized method for processing and measuring what they perceive as disorderly, uncertain, and elusive qualities. This process simplifies and mechanizes decision making, thus enabling the economists to avoid dealing with the complexities of development (1998).

Yet commensuration also carries significant costs, especially when applied to values that some deem intrinsic or priceless. Methods of commensuration such as cost-benefit analysis often use units of analysis that obscure the distributional effects of policies and "favor immediate benefits and distant costs over long-term benefits and immediate costs" (326). This is inherently a political process; it assumes that all value is relative and creates new social categories whose value is measured according to a standard metric. Because commensuration "transgresses deeply significant moral and cultural boundaries" (326), it is the basis for contestation between multiple interpretive frameworks for human rights.

Case Study: The Rights of People Living with HIV/AIDS

How a manager frames human-rights-related issues in a project's official documents—by using an intrinsic rationale or an instrumental one—can have substantial effects on which populations are targeted and how human rights violations are addressed. As an example, I describe two investment projects relating to HIV/AIDS control, prevention, or treatment: the Tuberculosis and HIV/AIDS Control Project in the Russian Federation (approved on April 3, 2003) and the HIV/AIDS Prevention and Control Project in St. Lucia in the Caribbean (approved on July 6, 2004). By the time both projects were approved, human rights thinking had begun to permeate discussion of the right to health. Nevertheless, there is a significant disparity between how, and the extent to which, each project explicitly framed HIV/AIDS as a human rights issue.

The link between HIV/AIDS and human rights is based on the right to health, which is codified in key international human rights legal documents.[25] The international guidelines on HIV/AIDS and human rights, established by what was then called the UN Commission on Human Rights, recommend "the need for intensified efforts to ensure universal respect for and observance of human rights and fundamental freedoms for all, to reduce vulnerability to HIV/AIDS and to prevent HIV/AIDS-related discrimination and stigma" (1997).[26] Thus the realization of rights for people living with HIV/AIDS (PLWHA) requires protection against stigma and discrimination with regard to access to health, education and social services, and the reduction of "vulnerability." Vulnerability refers to "the lack of power of individuals and communities to minimize or modulate their risk of exposure to HIV infection and, once infected, to receive adequate care and support" (Gruskin and Tarantola 2002).

Analysis of the project appraisal documents reveals two approaches to the human rights of PLWHA. The project in St. Lucia exemplified the legal dimension of the intrinsic frame by citing the country's human rights legal obligations and aiming to address discrimination, stigma, and vulnerability. The project's development objective was "targeting interventions at high risk groups and implementing non-targeted activities for the general population."[27] One of the four major goals was to "reduce the degree of stigma and discrimination associated with the disease." The project report provided no economic justification for pursuing this goal; it simply presented the goal as intrinsic to protecting the fundamental human rights of PLWHA. The project assessed progress toward this goal by measuring "accepting and non-discriminatory attitudes by the population towards victims of the disease in the workplace and in the community."[28] A search of the 106–page project document revealed twenty-two instances of the words "vulnerable" or "vulnerability," twenty of "discrimination," nineteen of "stigma," and five of "human right(s)."

In addition, the project explicitly aimed to strengthen St. Lucia's legal and regulatory framework, by "(i) ensuring all citizens the full benefits of

the civil, economic and social rights universally recognized as being important to people living with HIV/AIDS and to other vulnerable groups; and
(ii) ensuring the provision of services to all who need them."[29] It promised
assistance in the drafting of a new law that would ensure to PLWHA "full
equality and dignity under the law, without stigma or discrimination."[30] It
also included support for civil society and community initiatives to provide
effective monitoring and ensure the right to information.

In contrast, the project in Russia, though implicitly supporting the human rights of PLWHA, took a more instrumental approach.[31] Its objectives
were to contain the growth of the HIV/AIDS and tuberculosis epidemics in
the short run and reverse their growth in the medium term.[32] It explicitly
linked the objectives to target number seven of the UN Millennium Development Goals, which aims to halt and reverse the spread of HIV/AIDS by
2015.[33] Yet the project did not target reduction of stigma or discrimination,
which are key requirements for protecting the human rights of PLWHA. A
search of the 102–page project document revealed minimal emphasis on
these human-rights-related goals. The document included sixteen instances
of the word "vulnerable" or "vulnerability," but only two of "stigmatization"
(and no references to "stigma"), one of "human right(s)," and none of "discrimination." There was also no explicit recognition of the need to ensure
universal civil, economic, or social rights, as was mentioned in the St. Lucia
project document.

This analysis demonstrates how divergent interpretive frames can vari-
ously shape the design of projects on the same issue. It also suggests the
range of factors that may influence which frame is used. Drawing on an
intrinsic frame for addressing HIV/AIDS and human rights, the St. Lucia
project included components on reducing stigma and discrimination as well
as legal reforms for ensuring universal civil, economic, and social rights.
The Russian project, in contrast, emphasized prevention and control, while
also furnishing treatment for those infected. The absence of components on
stigma and discrimination in this project, and thus the decision not to frame
HIV/AIDS in human rights terms, could be for a number of reasons. One
may be that the team was dominated by employees who prefer a cost-benefit
analysis to a legal approach and who concluded that funds would be better
spent on other preventive interventions. Another reason for the disparity
between the projects is politics in the borrower countries, which can tran-

scend interpretive gaps. The Russian government viewed the human rights of PLWHA as a sensitive, politically charged issue that it preferred to avoid. Even if the St. Lucian government took the same view, Russia holds much more influence than St. Lucia over Bank project design because it is a major borrower from the Bank and not a country that the Bank wants to upset. There is also a significant contrast in U.S.-Russia and U.S.-St. Lucia relations, so the United States could have pressured the Bank's board to approve only a project that does not raise human rights concerns in Russia.

We see here the importance of evaluating each project and the human rights frame on its own terms, taking into account multiple factors such as the politics in the country involved and the orientations of the employees who designed the project. One should recognize that which approach is adopted significantly affects the design of the project and how it is implemented. But what happens when employees holding dissimilar interpretive frames are working on the same project? Is it possible to mediate among these differences when attempting to formulate an institutional approach to human rights?

Toward Reconciliation?

Is reconciliation possible among proponents of the divergent interpretive frames, or are the approaches incompatible? Are there any areas for compromise between economists, who may shun lawyers for lacking the practical ability to accommodate resource constraints; and lawyers, who may criticize economists for diluting the legal and moral power of human rights?

Reconciliation among seemingly competing frames requires that members of the communities bridge their interpretive gaps. One opportunity to do so is to seek individual translators—that is, actors or actor groups who can forge compromise across interpretive communities. These translators would seek a common language, rather than translation of all discourses into one language, which would result in "discursive hegemony" (Black 2001, 51). They would serve as intermediaries "who can easily move between layers [of experts, for instance] because they conceptualize the issue in more than one way" (Merry 2006b, 210).

In the context of the Bank, translators would likely have to come from within the ranks of the institution to win legitimacy among staff, and have significant decision-making power to influence overall institutional policy.

There are at least two potential translator groups. The first includes proponents of the moral dimension of the intrinsic frame, who promote universal ethical principles (deliberately not framed as legal rights) and often acknowledge the need to accommodate resource constraints and the institutional capacities of various countries. However, their conciliatory efforts have been limited by their small numbers and relative absence in the higher staff ranks of the Bank.

A second potential translator group is staff personnel having interdisciplinary backgrounds who can engage in dialogue with multiple professional communities and launch collaborative programs between them. However, these employees are also few in number and interspersed throughout the bureaucracy, thus making it difficult for them to join forces and form their own interpretive community. The small number of individuals who have succeeded in furthering this goal are responsible for several innovative programs that traverse disciplinary communities. One example is the Social Science and Policy Seminar Series, biweekly events jointly sponsored by the Social Development Department and the Development Economics Vice Presidency, aimed at promoting intellectual dialogue among staff by bringing in top scholars in the non-economic social sciences who can influence development policy. Initiatives such as the joint seminar series may result in encouraging conversation among employees with varying interpretive frames who would not otherwise have the opportunity to meet or share ideas.

The recent human rights initiative led by Bank lawyers (described later in this chapter) is another attempt to bridge disciplinary communities by reaching out to economists, who hold the most intellectual weight in the institution. It was initially led by an outside consultant funded by the Nordic countries, thus a person less influenced by the Bank's incentive system and better able to serve as a more effective translator. What remains unclear is whether the lawyers' reframing of values into the language of economics will lead to detrimental "translation effects" (Morgan 2003, 17). This means the approach may be perceived as belonging to one disciplinary community and not sufficiently "owned" by all staff, possibly leading to underimplementation. Since the initiative is in the early stages, one cannot yet determine whether it will truly lead to dialogue between competing interpretive frames or ultimately be subverted.

Recent Human Rights Initiative

The higher status of economic discourse over legal discourse was a critical factor in determining how the Legal Department would frame the human rights agenda after release of the 2006 Legal Opinion on Human Rights. Following general counsel Roberto Dañino's resignation in January 2006, internal advocates of human rights were left with a potentially influential legal opinion but no one to champion it. The opinion remained in limbo as members of the Legal Department disagreed on its status and hesitated to circulate the document throughout the rest of the Bank. The department's culture of secrecy manifested itself in limited distribution of the opinion as well as reluctance to discuss it openly even within the department. Nevertheless, a small number of lawyers continued their efforts to push the human rights agenda forward.

In late 2005 and 2006, an informal group of lawyers (many of whom would help draft the 2006 legal opinion) began to organize activities toward furthering the human rights agenda and taking an explicit approach to human rights. A prominent member of the group was a senior lawyer from the Danish Ministry of Foreign Affairs who was hired in October 2005 by the Legal Department. His appointment was funded by the Nordic countries, which have demonstrated strong support for a human rights agenda despite opposition from other members of the Board of Executive Directors.[34] On October 20, 2005, the Nordic countries presented a working paper to President Wolfowitz entitled "The World Bank and Human Rights."[35] The paper discussed "why and how the human rights perspective should be enhanced in the World Bank's policies and operations with a view to reinforcing its development and poverty eradication mission."[36] It opened a dialogue on human rights with Wolfowitz and became part of a new Nordic-and-Baltic-sponsored initiative, which was an attempt to finally bring the issue of human rights out of the closet.

As its first order of business, the initiative proposed creating the Justice and Human Rights Trust Fund, whose purpose was "to provide effective support . . . to include human rights considerations in the analytical and operational activities of the World Bank Group."[37] Activities were to include empirical research, country case studies, and outreach across the Bank through human rights education and training of operations staff. The trust fund would be managed by the Legal Vice Presidency (in cooperation with representatives from other Bank units), be funded by the Nordic countries, and have a minimum life span of five years.

Internal politics and a collapse in leadership after the resignation of Wolfowitz prevented launching the Justice and Human Rights Trust Fund until 2009, when it was renamed the Nordic Trust Fund under the management of the Bank's Operations Policy and Country Services network.[38] The deliberations I witnessed in 2006 on the objectives and activities of the trust fund suggest possible ways to operationalize human rights norms at the Bank. While they were designing the trust fund's plan of action, the lawyers faced resistance and had to revise their approach to adapt it to the Bank's organizational culture. Their recent efforts address (or, at times, sidestep) several institutional obstacles that plagued prior efforts to introduce human rights, among them lack of a pragmatic orientation, failure to conduct outreach to the staff in headquarters and the country offices, limited resources, and fear on the part of the Board of Executive Directors and senior management that adopting human rights was too controversial and beyond the Bank's mandate.

Framing Human Rights for Economists

One of the main components of the lawyers' strategy was an attempt to frame human rights for the economists who dominated the Bank. In carrying out social change, activists often use a mechanism of framing issues to resonate with the interests, ideologies, and cultural understandings of their target audience (see Snow and Benford 1992; Benford and Snow 2000). Framing is part of a process of meaning making that is central to social movements. It entails "the strategic creation and manipulation of shared understandings and interpretations of the world, its problems, and viable courses of action" (Campbell 2005, 49). In the process, norms are translated to fit the dominant cultural understandings within the institution.

The lawyers who helped draft the 2006 legal opinion recognized the interpretive gap between their vision of human rights and that of the economists. They spoke with employees in headquarters and the field offices who questioned the added value of a human rights approach in comparison to existing good practices, which already incorporated some human rights principles albeit implicitly. Throughout these discussions, they encountered a need for more empirical work to demonstrate the causal links between human rights and economic growth. Some employees complained of a lack of clarity over what is meant by a rights-based approach to development. Would it simply be a rhetorical repackaging of existing practice? Many staff members also perceived human rights norms as overly rigid, particularly when defined with respect to international legal instruments, leaving little room for the trade-offs that are often necessary in development practice.

As the lawyers debated how to design the new trust fund, they were torn over whether an instrumental approach would dilute the intrinsic meaning of human rights and worried about the risk of taking an overly technical approach to rights. Despite their misgivings, the lawyers decided to pursue a strategy of "economizing human rights" (see Morgan 2003). Economizing human rights refers to an effort to demystify the concept and build a constituency among staff while promoting an empirical approach that quantitatively measures human rights performance.

According to a senior Bank economist, "We will not make inroads in the Bank if [human rights] language is not made into economic language without compromising the substance."[39] This statement suggests the importance of translating human rights into the dominant discourse of economics, yet it also raises the question of whether this strategy does indeed dilute (or even strip) human rights of its core substance. The decision to economize human rights was a pragmatic one. The lawyers recognized that past attempts to introduce the agenda failed in part because they had neglected to build a constituency at the Bank. Here is a statement by another Bank economist emphasizing the value of empirical evidence in furthering agendas within the institution such as anticorruption:

> I think that things really happen in the Bank when an economic case could be made for them. You put [them] in economic language. This is how corruption came in. It sort of became acceptable internally to talk about corruption when people could show with cross-country regressions that it's related to lower growth. . . . People needed [economic-based evidence] to say that, "OK, it's all right for us to work on this." So one obstacle would be to try and articulate rights issues in the way that economists could understand.[40]

As part of an attempt to speak to economists, the lawyers adopted a largely instrumental approach to rights in the proposed Justice and Human Rights Trust Fund.

One of the trust fund's main objectives was to "serve as a hub for bol-
stering an emerging community of practice around human rights in the
Bank."[41] In preparation for the trust fund, the Norwegian government financed a workshop on May 15–16, 2006. The topic was developing indicators for "measuring justice" so as to evaluate the performance of a country's
justice sector.[42] The workshop also discussed the Legal Department's project on human rights indicators, which had begun in 2005 and was developed in collaboration with the Danish Institute for Human Rights. As part
of this empirical focus, the lawyers planned to pilot projects in borrower
countries and thereby shift the focus of implementation to countries rather
than the headquarters. Pilot projects would also allow them to empirically
study the effects of using a human rights approach in Bank projects.

Operating "Under the Radar":
Pursuing Pilot Projects Rather Than a Policy

> The trouble with the Bank is that getting anything adopted as an institutional
> position or strategy is really tough because . . . there's been a shift towards
> decentralizing things. So getting to a policy is almost the last step after things
> have already percolated [within the institution]. It's almost like practice pre-
> cedes policy in this place. . . . Back in the 1990s, it was the opposite way—
> that if you wanted to get something done, you would push the policy first,
> and then practice would follow. For example, the safeguard policies. Those
> were key to getting people to change behavior. It's kind of the opposite now.
> [Changes in] behavior tend to happen through pilot projects.[43]

After years of internal and external advocacy for an institutional policy on
human rights, internal advocates began moving toward a country-level approach. The lawyers who designed the trust fund decided that the Bank's
country staff should take the lead on any human rights initiative, with support from the donor community. They considered regional and national
ownership critical to a successful human rights agenda. They advanced as
one reason for this tactic the significant decision-making role that country
directors play at the Bank, "much more so than vice presidents, . . . and certainly much more so than sector directors or sector managers. [They are the
ones] who are really making the decisions in terms of resource allocation,
and are leading the dialogue with the country."[44]

One of the trust fund's preparatory workshops focused on country-level initiatives, including pilot projects, integration of human rights principles into national development strategies, and promotion of human rights dialogues with national authorities.[45] There was also a proposal that human rights be incorporated into the poverty-reduction strategy papers of governments that requested assistance in integrating human rights concerns into their development strategies. The Bank would then assist those governments in "translating internationally agreed human rights standards into operational policy actions, thereby prioritizing support for those services that both contribute to economic and social development and constitute human rights obligations on the state."[46] Yet human rights programming would be limited to those borrower countries requesting to incorporate human rights concerns into their development strategies. Under the proposal, it would not be used as a conditionality on aid.

The team of lawyers behind the recent approach made a strategic decision to focus on pilot projects rather than advocate for a stand-alone operational policy. One reason for this decision was the previously discussed staff incentive system, in which internal promotions are based on lending targets rather than compliance with safeguard policies. Several staff members I interviewed expressed general resentment of the existing policies, as seen in this statement: "People [have been] feeling that the compliance police are after them, and that the procedures are rigid and bureaucratic. . . . And there [is] a lot of weariness from the experience of the safeguards about trying to make things mandatory because it'll be seen as a burden. So the idea is trying to do this through good practice examples."[47] Another reason for the pilot project approach was that the lawyers recognized the board would not approve a new policy at the time, owing to internal divisions. As a result, they chose to pursue an incremental strategy of working under the board's radar screen.

An incremental, under-the-radar strategy stands in contrast to one of mainstreaming, which entails explicit management support for incorporating an issue into existing programs. Prior mainstreaming occurred at the Bank when environmental concerns were incorporated into its programming through adoption of an operational policy on environmental assessment.[48] Yet to introduce a more sensitive and controversial issue such as human rights, internal advocates espoused a strategy of implicit manage-

ment support and avoidance of the board. A senior advisor to an executive director acknowledged the value of an incremental strategy for human
rights, observing that Bank officials "shouldn't try and get a formal process
going because it would backfire and that [they] should basically do a human
rights agenda through stealth."[49] The executive director of the Bank's Nordic
Baltic office agreed. He explained that trust funds are a way to introduce
controversial changes into the Bank because they do not require board approval: "The strategy is to hurry slowly, below the radar."[50]

Conclusion

As the group of lawyers pursue an incremental, economistic human rights
strategy, internal struggles persist in the Legal Department and among the
lawyers themselves over how to define and frame human rights. Many wel-
come an economic framing as the only entry point to bringing human rights
into the institution. However, they are also concerned that human rights be
used "in the right way," referring to a legalistic interpretation.[51] They recognize there are risks in taking an overly technical approach to rights, one
that uses empirical tools such as indicators and checklists. Several lawyers
who support the pragmatic approach also insist that it "is essential . . . that
efforts to integrate human rights in development practice not compromise
those key characteristics [of legal obligations and duties] in the process, and
risk the impoverishment of rights discourse and the undermining of core
values and objectives that human rights were conceived to realize" (Decker,
McInerney-Lankford, and Sage 2005, 49). Yet they did not specify how this
could be achieved.

The internal struggles among lawyers and in the Legal Department reveal
a tension between principles and pragmatism, between pursuing normative,
intangible values and goals on the one hand and finding a practical approach
for solving problems (which may make it necessary to reconcile competing
principles) on the other. In an environment like the Bank where most issues are subject to cost-benefit analysis, employees may be ambivalent about
principles that appear to be nonnegotiable or subject to trade-offs. They may
perceive potential costs in trying to render commensurate seemingly incommensurable values. In her analysis of the struggle over a dam in Arizona
between Yavapai Indians and the Bureau of Reclamation, Wendy Espeland
explained that an attempt to translate land into a substantive rationality led

to political resistance from the Yavapai and reinterpretation of their collective identity (1998). In the context of the Bank, the conflict over economizing human rights has led to reevaluation of professional identities, particularly among lawyers who were torn between their allegiance to the legal principles in which they were trained and the economic values privileged at the Bank.

The conflict over human rights has also uncovered internal battles over the institution's own identity and how broadly one could interpret the Bank's mandate of poverty reduction. Advocates for issues that are new to the Bank have attempted to frame them as more pragmatic and measurable, in line with the mainstream economic development goals of the Bank. For example, Bank sociologists and anthropologists in the late 1990s and early 2000s decided to package the concept of social capital in an economic framework to give it legitimacy. Yet in doing so, many of them struggled with the tension between principles and pragmatism. They looked for a concept that "could readily engage in conversations with the economic arguments underpinning much of the Bank's activity" (Bebbington et al. 2004, 42). They felt that if the social capital concept could be quantified and discussed econometrically, it could bridge the gap between social development specialists and economists. But as with the debate over how to frame human rights, several non-economists critiqued this approach. They argued that converting social capital into a quantifiable asset "independent of the broader political economy does unacceptable violence to any concept of social relationships" (46). They debated such questions as, Would mainstreaming the concept dilute it and cause irreparable damage? If so, is this an acceptable cost since it may be the only way to introduce social issues into an economist-dominated institution like the Bank?

Here we see the possible risks of translating human rights too far into the existing power structure. As Sally Engle Merry observed, if human rights "are translated so fully that they blend into existing power relationships completely, they lose their potential for social change" (2006b, 135–36). This is part of the dilemma of human rights framing and "vernacularization" strategies: they will not induce radical, long-term change if they do not challenge existing power structures and are too compatible with dominant ways of thinking (2006b). Nevertheless, they also need to resonate with local cultural understandings in order to appear legitimate and become part of local rights consciousness (2006b).

This conundrum raises important questions: Can human rights be so extensively vernacularized that they lose their essential core, or even contradict their fundamental meanings? Must human rights remain connected to a legal regime (and be linked to state obligations deriving from international law) to continue to be considered "human rights" and not another concept such as "empowerment"? In the concluding chapter, I further explore these questions, situate them within existing scholarship, and suggest possible areas for future research.

Chapter 5

Conclusion

THE DILEMMA OF HUMAN RIGHTS at the World Bank is a microcosm through which to study the negotiation of competing values within a global governance institution. This book begins with the problem of why the Bank has not adopted a human rights policy or agenda despite a number of factors that favor doing so, including internal and external pressure over the past two decades as well as the agency's own pro-human-rights rhetoric. The answer to this puzzle lies in the Bank's organizational culture, which is ideologically and discursively framed in such a way that its employees have resisted engaging with human rights in their work. Existing theories behind the marginality of human rights at the institution focus exclusively on the legal restrictions in its Articles of Agreement and the politics among member countries on its Board of Executive Directors. I argue that this approach has underemphasized the internal dynamics within the bureaucracy, including the production and circulation of knowledge and the interaction among professional groups whose actions may depart from the interests of member states. A variety of ambiguities imbue the Bank's organizational life: among them, slippage between the institution's official mission and multiple implicit mandates, clashes between domains of expertise, and ethical dilemmas among employees as they negotiate competing value spheres such as human rights and economics.

My study demonstrates that human rights is a substantive value that challenges the Bank's dominant regime of economic knowledge. I uncover a clash of rationalities—the market versus social democratic liberalism, the latter into which human rights nestles—and internal contestation over the legitimacy of human rights as a normative technology in an increasingly bureaucratized world. When bureaucratized, rights can become subordinated to the forms and logics of the market. In the case of the World Bank, their political potential to challenge state sovereignty and bring about social justice has been curtailed. In other words, the Bank's depoliticizing apparatus has shaped the diffusion of human rights within the institution by emphasizing its regulatory dimension (including its instrumental, rule-oriented, and administrative qualities) and disregarding its sovereignty dimension (which invokes its universal character, symbolic valence, and emancipatory power).

In the last chapter, I described how internal advocates have met with early success in mainstreaming human rights, but only after they defined it under an instrumental framework and introduced it incrementally through country-based pilot projects. This recent initiative by members of the Legal Department offers insights into the critical bureaucratic obstacles that have impeded human rights internalization, including a clash of expertise among staff and the Bank's incentive system. Internal advocates have attempted to appeal to the dominant subculture of economists by framing human rights as quantifiable and instrumentally valuable in achieving the economic development goals of the Bank. They have pursued an incremental strategy from the bottom up through country-level pilot projects, rather than a top-down operational policy that would require board approval. By late 2006, this strategy became public and was no longer under the radar (see Palacio 2006), but it is too early to fully gauge success.

I argue that there are costs of imbuing rights with a functionalist orientation and subduing its sovereignty dimension. If the political potential is negated, human rights may lose its essential core and be rendered impotent. Is this what is happening at the Bank, in light of the recent strategy of "economizing" and thus depoliticizing and delegalizing human rights? What are the unintended consequences of infusing normative values such as human rights with an instrumental logic? The long-term costs are difficult to measure at this time, but the case of mainstreaming (and depoliticizing) anticorruption at the Bank suggests possible implications for the future of human rights. Though a comprehensive analysis is beyond the scope of this book, I will briefly review the history of the anticorruption agenda at the Bank and highlight possible similarities to human rights.

Lessons from the Mainstreaming of Anticorruption in the World Bank

Until the mid-1990s, the issue of corruption at the Bank had a history similar to that of human rights. Activities such as addressing corruption in the Bank's projects or refusing to lend money to corrupt regimes were interpreted as contrary to its Articles of Agreement; like human rights, corruption was viewed as too political and thus beyond the Bank's mandate, which requires lending to be based solely on economic considerations.

Yet a sea change occurred as a result of both external and internal pressure. Critics challenged the Bank's neoliberal policies, as exemplified by its failed structural adjustment and shock therapy programs, while donor states demanded greater accountability for development projects. An internal battle also occurred, along with a paradigm shift within economic theory toward a greater role for the state in creating and monitoring institutions (Weaver 2008). Internal support for governance issues was slowly developing; the most critical breakthrough occurred after James Wolfensohn assumed the presidency in 1995. He announced his intention to tackle the "cancer of corruption" in a 1996 speech at the Bank's annual meeting. The following year, the Bank released its first strategy report on the issue and announced it would establish a "systematic framework for addressing corruption as a development issue in the assistance it provides to countries and in its operational work more generally" (World Bank 1997, 2).

A prerequisite for the Bank's explicit embrace of the anticorruption and governance agenda was depoliticization and translation into an economic logic. Bank employees produced economic research that established the negative development outcomes of corrupt regimes while largely avoiding overtly political issues, such as election processes and the financing of political parties (Marquette 2004). The Bank also described its new focus on anticorruption as "demand-driven" in order to deflect criticism that it was interfering in member countries' political affairs (2004). As with the case of human rights, there was internal resistance to an economic approach to corruption, both from skeptical employees who feared the slippery slope of the Bank overstretching its mandate and from staff members who criticized the institution for not addressing the political aspects of governance. Yet this resistance had little impact on the institution's mainstream policies.

At this point, the story of corruption looks similar to that of human rights. But in the case of corruption, we have the luxury of more than ten years of experience to reflect on the effects of stripping the issue of its political dimensions. The Bank has mainstreamed a limited definition of corruption, including a false dichotomy between politics and administration that assumes a distinction between bureaucratic corruption and political corruption (Polzer 2001). This interpretation has resulted in a gap between ideology and operations as well as an implementation of the agenda that is flawed at best and destructive to the Bank's mission at worst. As one scholar has noted: "[The Bank's] anti-corruption activities have been tentative and confused, demanding that national governments be seen to be doing something about corruption and supporting investigations into fraud, and then pulling away at the last minute when the investigations bear fruit. It issues statements about unacceptable high-level corruption, while distancing itself from the leadership changes and political turmoil that result" (Marquette 2004, 426). Despite significant operational changes, including new policies and creation of departments dedicated to governance issues, the process of mainstreaming anticorruption remains "contested and incomplete" (Weaver 2008, 91).

It has been difficult to implement the agenda without directly addressing the political environments of states within which corruption flourishes. The Bank's economic model of corruption has resulted in misallocation of staff resources by "precluding the perceived need to hire more social scientists and to develop the policy tools and skill sets necessary to address the *political* economy of governance reform" (114). In 2001, the Bank's Operations Evaluation Department recognized the operational implications of the institution's depoliticization of corruption: "Good governance is the product of complex political, social, economic, and cultural factors. Good analysis of governance problems requires skills in all these areas. However, to date, the Bank is preeminently an organization of economists and is dominated by economic thinking. . . . The Bank's handful of political scientists are largely marginalized" (World Bank 2001, 54; quoted in Weaver 2008, 116).

The lack of appropriately skilled staff has resulted in projects neglecting the unquantifiable aspects of governance that may be critical for addressing the deep causes of corruption and instituting effective reform. Former President Paul Wolfowitz recognized the gap between rhetoric and reality when he prioritized anticorruption during his brief tenure. His efforts to close the gap, however, through such means as increasing professional expertise and strengthening the Bank's Department of Institutional Integrity, met with limited success in light of distrust of Wolfowitz among staff and member countries and the personal scandals that led to his eventual resignation in 2007.

What lessons can we gather for the future of human rights? Depoliticizing value-laden issues such as corruption or human rights may be a necessary first step for their eventual mainstreaming into an economic institution like the Bank. However, as we see in the case of corruption, an economic model that ignores political dimensions will not achieve desired long-term development outcomes and will undermine the legitimacy and influence of the Bank. Now that human rights is losing its taboo status and beginning to enter the institution through an instrumental framework, I contend that it will one day have to be repoliticized (i.e., the sovereignty dimension will need to be recognized and addressed) before real organizational change can occur.

Toward a Risk Management Approach to Human Rights?

Human rights is a difficult agenda to incorporate into an economic institution because it may lead employees to face a struggle between principles and pragmatism. Some critics fear that although legalizing human rights norms may limit their persuasiveness within the Bank, an economic framework would dilute their meaning and serve as a ceiling for comparable standards within other development agencies. Thus another extension of my research is the role of human rights in other international financial institutions and private organizations, particularly multinational corporations.

In response to growing concern over corporate social responsibility, some companies are beginning to address human rights beyond mere lip service. What is notable is that, like the World Bank, they have framed human rights norms in an economic manner that adapts to their business model. In doing so, they have adopted a risk-based approach that defines human rights violations as not only ethical dilemmas but also strategic risks, which may damage a company's reputation and public image, threaten profits, and possibly lead to litigation. For instance, companies such as Novartis and Heineken have adopted human rights compliance assessments and country risk indicators.

The Danish Institute for Human Rights (a national human rights institution founded in 1987) has been a prominent player in promoting this pragmatic, business-friendly approach to human rights through the Human Rights and Business Project, launched in 1999. The Danish Institute operates at the juncture between the business community and the international human rights community. It has developed a hybrid economic-legal framework for corporate social responsibility, one that is based on human rights norms delineated in international legal instruments but that also notably applies a risk-management framework responsive to companies' economic efficiency concerns. The toolkit includes country human rights risk assessments, a country commitment index (a scoring of implementation of human rights legislation), an online corporate social responsibility compass (for small and medium-sized companies to address human rights in global supply chains), and a human rights hotline. In this way, human rights is becoming another area subject to risk-based regulation (see Sunstein 2002; Breyer 1993; Pildes and Sunstein 1995).

As risk management becomes increasingly common in private and public governance (see Power 2004), what does it mean if it is now being applied to human rights? On the one hand, such an approach is operational, contextual, and nonlegalistic, so it may appeal to business-oriented employees. It could incentivize actors to go beyond compliance and innovate as a way to enhance their competitive advantage. It can also be implemented as part of companies' overall risk management systems (already addressing financial, safety, and environmental risks), which have become widespread since the passing of the Sarbanes-Oxley Act of 2002. Moreover, a risk management approach may lend support to cross-institutional standard-setting initiatives on human rights, thus enabling greater partnerships and consistency (e.g., among private banks, international organizations, export credit agencies, and corporations). Finally, one could argue that human rights law is already replete with risk concerns and instrumental rationales—an example being balancing of the right against torture and risks to national security—so this approach is consistent with existing practice.

On the other hand, there may be unintended consequences in a risk management approach to human rights, especially given that the concept of risk is relative and politically contested. Voluntary initiatives that rely on internal monitoring systems with no reporting requirements may create opportunities to weaken or avoid human rights standards (see Minow 2003).[1] A related concern also suggested by my study of the World Bank is whether issues such as human rights can indeed be quantified, and what is lost in the process.

Future research can explore the unintended consequences of a risk-based/economic approach to human rights as well as the process of diffusion of international norms within private institutions. There are few empirical studies that look inside corporations to understand how human rights are being integrated into business decision making, including how corporations are integrating human rights principles within their risk management systems and adapting them to suit their unique risk appetites and organizational cultures. Why are particular organizations such as the Danish Institute for Human Rights serving as translators between divergent normative discourses and as intermediaries between actors? How are corporate actors conceiving of human rights risks? Is there a tension among the corporate lawyer's roles as risk manager, compliance officer, and advocate? As my research on the culture of the Bank's Legal Department demonstrates, lawyers are increasingly confronting ethical challenges in their work. With the globalization of markets and the offshoring of legal services, corporate lawyers have to manage transborder issues and operate across legal systems. They must tackle challenges similar to those faced by Bank lawyers, such as corruption by governments, civil unrest, and disputes over labor and human rights. Therefore it would be important to examine ethnographically the changing role of the legal profession within global organizations.

Implications

This study has implications for a range of audiences interested in human rights, international lawmaking, and institutions of global governance. Next I provide an overview of how this study seeks to contribute to literature in these fields.

The Anthropology of Human Rights and International Law

My research is informed by, and seeks to contribute to, anthropological literature on human rights and international law. Anthropology's relationship with human rights has significantly evolved from a preoccupation with the universalism-versus cultural-relativism debate (see An-Na'im 1992). There are a number of critical themes raised in contemporary anthropological literature. Analyzing human rights as both discourse and social practice, scholars have studied the process of producing and translating norms as well as how those norms become meaningful on the ground. They have adopted a discursive approach that "radically decenters international human rights law" and assumes that "social practice is, in part, constitutive of the idea of human rights itself" (Goodale 2007, 8; see also Baxi 2002). Recent work has also examined how human rights become vernacularized in local settings as they are appropriated and then translated into local terms (Merry 2006a). Some scholars have analyzed human rights as a disciplinary knowledge practice and uncovered the technocratic and instrumental approach of human rights practitioners (Riles 2006). Others have studied the impact of human rights discourse on local social and political contexts, whether in a community or an international institution. Such studies examine the interaction and possible conflicts between human rights discourse and other global normative discourses, such as those of justice or human dignity (Rajagopal 2007).

My study contributes to existing scholarship that has uncovered the plural nature of the human rights framework and explored translation of the framework into local contexts. The fragmented character of human rights is due to its multiple and sometime contradictory roles: as a tool of empowerment for weak, dispossessed individuals; as a unifying message for social movements; and as a symbol of the U.S.-led neoliberal project. As Austin Sarat and Thomas Kearns observed, "The allure of human rights persists because they can, and do, mean many things at once. . . . They both constitute us as subjects and provide a language through which we can resist that constitution and forge new identities" (2001, 6–7). When human rights norms are localized, they are not just transplanted but are adapted and vernacularized in a variety of ways (Merry 2006b). To develop local rights consciousness among groups and individuals, rights must fit within or among existing normative frameworks (An-Na'im 1992; Merry 2006b). This fit may occur through a process of layering, where a rights framework exists alongside other sets of ideas such as kinship obligations (Merry 2006b). The central actors in the process are the "translators," or "people who can move between layers because they conceptualize the issue in more than one way" (2006b, 210). These intermediaries may, for example, be local activists or transnational lawyers who translate human rights concepts to those at the grassroots level and translate local perspectives back up to the international level.

However, there are limits to vernacularization, for instance when human rights contradict local conceptions of justice and security (Wilson 2007). Asserting human rights could be costly if doing so challenges local social norms (Merry 2006b). According to Sally Engle Merry's study of indigenous women in rural Hong Kong, assertions of their right to gender equality and thus their right to inherit family land challenged local obligations of kinship and community as well as Chinese customary law, which forbade female inheritance (ibid.). This raises a paradox in the vernacularization process. Human rights frequently need to resonate with local cultural understandings (including institutional and national cultures) if they are to be accepted by community members. At the same time, they must often reflect universal principles if they are to establish their legitimacy and maintain their transformative character (2006b).

My research extends these ideas by revealing another limit of vernacularization: the critical costs that ensue when translation goes too far. I describe how Bank lawyers have recently translated human rights into an economic framework to resonate with the disciplinary group that is dominant within the institution. They have thus attempted to depoliticize rights by vacating their emancipatory dimension, including their normative valence and legal framework. The strategy of "economizing" human rights has internally divided Bank lawyers, some of whom fear that it impoverishes the rights discourse and undermines its core values.

The process of translating human rights raises another important concern: Where does law fit in? Existing literature has frequently distinguished between human rights law and human rights discourse, "where the former refers to positivised rules in national or international law and the latter refers to how people speak about those norms, or aspire to expand or interpret them in new ways" (Wilson 2007, 350). Anthropologists have studied the process by which moral claims are channeled as legal claims against state governments. Some scholars contend that this legalization process is not indeed transformative since claimants must rely on the state-based international human rights system (2007). Others emphasize how this process is a politically contested one, for example, how the complex drafting of a new international legal instrument can result in ambiguities, silences, and contradictions (Warren 1997).

My research confirms the anthropological insight that human rights law is distinct from human rights discourse, but it also further unpacks the dimensions of human rights law to reveal a gap between the symbolic valence of law as a political concept and the codified version that is susceptible to being instrumentalized. In an approach similar to that for human rights, the Bank has attempted to depoliticize law by embracing its instrumental characteristics—thus engaging law in the service of other values such as economic growth and efficiency. For instance, legal and judicial reform projects aim to enforce the rule of law in order to reduce bureaucratic harassment, strengthen property rights and institutions, facilitate private investment, and thus contribute to economic performance. Yet again, as with human rights, the Bank has not embraced law's political dimension and capability to engender radical change and justice.

Given the legal character of human rights, anthropological debate on this subject is closely related to that on international law. With the recent creation of new global legal institutions, new forms of global law, and transnational social movements around legal issues, anthropologists are studying the multiplicity of sites where international law operates in practice (Merry 2006a). Scholars have analyzed the practices of international courts and international tribunals and their conceptions of justice in relation to those of local communities (e.g., Wilson 2001 on the South African Truth and Reconciliation Commission; Clarke 2009 on the International Criminal Court). They have studied the global impact of law-oriented nongovernmental organizations on postcolonial consciousness (John L. Comaroff and Jean Comaroff 2006). They have also analyzed the production of international treaties by transnational elites and their localization and translation on the ground (e.g., Merry 2006b on the Convention on the Elimination of All Forms of Discrimination Against Women, or CEDAW; Warren 2007 on the UN's Human Trafficking Protocol). With the continued expansion of international law, there is a growing need for anthropologists to continue uncovering how it is produced and operates in practice.

The World Bank has emerged as an important actor in the international law community since its founding in 1944. It exercises political and economic leverage over countries through loan and credit agreements, which are binding under the international law of treaties (Boisson de Chazournes 2000). Because it conditions these agreements on compliance with operational standards, the Bank can incorporate specific policy and institutional reforms into domestic legal systems. By exerting control over the policies of borrower countries, the Bank plays a vital role in the internalization and domestic enforcement of international law. As an international organization, the Bank is more than just a collection of individual member states; it also serves as a governance institution with its own international legal personality. This status as a legal person means the Bank can both execute and be subject to international responsibilities and obligations, possibly including obligations incumbent on it under international agreements and customary international law. In its analysis of the culture of the Bank, this book reveals the competing subcultures and other internal contestations that may impede the internationalization of norms and their application in member states.

The study of international law has also brought renewed interest in theories of legal pluralism to understand local settings where multiple legal orders interact. Scholars such as Francis Snyder and Sally Engle Merry have introduced analytic frameworks for understanding transnational lawmaking. Snyder studied the international trade in toys between the European Union (EU) and China as a global economic network of legal sites, including the European Union, the World Trade Organization, and multinational corporations (1999). According to Snyder, "global legal pluralism" described the interaction of EU law, U.S. law, WTO law, Chinese law, codes of conduct from multinational corporations and trade associations, and international customs and conventions. He defined *global legal pluralism* as a network of interwoven sets of norms (Snyder 1999). Building upon this work, Merry proposed a "spatial global legal pluralism," which "incorporates dimensions of power, meaning, and social relationships into a legal pluralist framework along with an analysis of spatial relationships" (2008, 151). This version of legal pluralism conceptualizes the spatial dimensions of laws in order to analyze their transnational movement and the places where they intersect, overlap, and conflict. It is a theoretically rich framework for understanding "the way pockets of legal regimes jump to new regions through transplants, global legal institutions, ratification of human rights treaties, the creation of special tribunals, and myriad other processes" (164). I build on this framework by analyzing the regulatory mechanisms and power relations that shape these legal terrains. I specifically focus on the dynamics of legal plural-ism that operate within an international institution that both creates interna-tional law and shapes domestic law. In doing so, I adopt the cautionary tone of Kamari Clarke in her critique of legal pluralist theories: "Approaches that downplay uneven relations in the process of lawmaking or the politics of in-commensurability surrounding the basis for deriving justice undermine the relevance of power and hegemony in shaping the conditions of the possible, in shaping the conditions for imagining 'justice'" (2009, 119).

My research on the Bank contributes to the anthropology of inter-national law in a variety of ways. Various epistemic communities interact around the institution (including state government representatives, civil so-ciety advocates, and local communities), but the Bank always controls the terms of their engagement. This is the reason I focus on the internal dynam-ics within the bureaucracy, including the making of policy, the movement of ideas, the production and circulation of knowledge, and the interaction between professional groups. I emphasize employees' varied systems of meaning and ways of defining problems, which structure how development projects are designed and implemented and thus how the institution ad-dresses global poverty. This approach highlights how micropolitics within global legal institutions can shape international policy and state practice, while concurrently being shaped by the global political landscape. It reveals the everyday decision-making processes of bureaucrats and also uncovers their autonomy and discretion in influencing institutional practice in ways that depart from the interests of member states.

When the issue of human rights intersects with the Bank, the institution becomes a site of legal pluralism—a setting where institutional norms, inter-national legal norms, and domestic norms overlap and possibly conflict. For instance, a Bank economist carrying out a health project in Kenya may con-front a conflict over how to implement a component on sexual and repro-ductive health. She may have to consider whether and how to reconcile Bank norms (as defined by the institution's operational policies), international human rights norms on women and health (as defined by the UN), and cultural and domestic legal norms from Kenya. To understand the power relationships between multiple norms and how employees address possible conflicts between them, we must analyze the Bank as a site not only of legal pluralism but also of discursive pluralism (the interaction between multiple and at times competing discourses, which themselves are situated within a broader field of power relations) and interpretive pluralism (the interaction between multiple interpretations of discourses, legal and otherwise).

I agree with other anthropologists that the human rights framework is plural in its conceptualization (Wilson 2006a), but what have been underemphasized are the power dynamics between the human rights discourse and other discourses, and especially between human rights interpretations themselves. Multiple discourses and their related agendas have entered the Bank over the past two decades—gender, corruption, and the environment, to name but a few. According to some employees, these discourses may operate in tension with the Bank's dominant discourse of economic development, whose meaning is contested not only among states but also within the institution itself. Whether these discourses are commensurable or not, and how they interact, depends on how they are interpreted. According to my research, the interpretation in turn depends on a number of factors, including ideological differences and the expert cultures of employees (see Knorr-Cetina 1999). Are the discourses of human rights and development reconcilable? An economist, a lawyer, and a sociologist may respond differently, on the basis of their professional training and their respective definitions of human rights and development. Moreover, a civil society advocate lobbying the Bank or an executive director on its board may hold distinct interpretations as well.

I contend that the power relationships between interpretations depend on the institutional and social context where human rights are being situated. My research particularly focuses on the interpretive pluralism of human rights among bureaucrats—that is, the potential conflict between an intrinsic rationale (both in legal and moral terms) and an instrumental rationale (in economic terms) for human rights, both of which closely correspond to the professional background of employees (e.g., lawyers and economists, respectively). This conflict reinforces the anthropological insight that human rights law is but one manifestation of the human rights concept.

The Study of International Institutions and Global Governance

By analyzing the culture of an international economic institution through the lens of a universal discourse, I seek to uncover the dynamics of global norm making and the politics of negotiation and contestation (among experts and member states as well as ideologies) within international organizations (IOs). In so doing, this research can inform scholars in international relations (IR) and international law who study norm diffusion and institutions of global governance.

Existing scholarship in these fields has understudied the norm dynamics that operate within IOs and overemphasized the role of states in shaping IO behavior. The rational-actor theories that have historically dominated international relations—realism and functionalism—are largely state-centric in their analyses of how IOs behave (see, e.g., Keohane 1984; Waltz 1979). They do not account for agency autonomy that departs from the interests and power of member governments (see Nielson and Tierney 2003). According to these theories, IOs are solely agents of their member states and their actions always reflect the power distribution among those states. IOs play a larger role in the models developed by neoliberals and institutionalists, who focus on the actions and interests of individuals, interest groups, and political institutions that shape state preferences.

Constructivist accounts have further departed from traditional IR theory by providing more autonomy to IOs, which serve as vehicles by which states are socialized into complying with norms (see, e.g., Ruggie 1998; Wendt 1992). For instance, transnational advocacy networks can influence state behavior by appealing to IOs, which then pressure member states to implement norms in their domestic systems (see Keck and Sikkink 1998). Constructivists have also analyzed IOs as bureaucracies, with their own internal logic, behavioral proclivities, and pathologies (Barnett and Finnemore 2004). In this way, IOs are "authorities in their own right" and are attentive to not only state interests but their own interests as well (ibid. 5). They are constitutive of actors (e.g., states, NGOs, and individuals) while also being constituted by them. Yet even though constructivists have moved international relations away from state-centric theories and toward an understanding of their internal workings, they are only beginning to offer empirical accounts of IO behavior.

Most existing case studies of IOs by political scientists do not comprehensively analyze the organizational cultures of IOs, which can be understood only through long-term participant observation and in-depth interviews. My study of the World Bank seeks to contribute to this literature and inspire more ethnographic analyses of IO behavior, which are critical for explaining why and how organizations change. I have demonstrated that institutions can have relative autonomy even when member states hold competing preferences and do not reach consensus. In these circumstances, IO officials have discretion and can significantly influence how institutions behave.

My research also contributes to the emerging trend in legal scholarship toward an interdisciplinary approach to international law and institutions that is based on empirical research methodologies. This study highlights the importance of qualitative data based on ethnographic fieldwork, which challenges document-oriented legal analyses of the infiltration of norms into international organizations. Most existing theories of international law, like those in international relations, fail to peel back the layers of IOs far enough to reveal the inner workings and decision-making processes. Though legal scholars increasingly treat IOs as their object of study (see, e.g., Alvarez 2005; Sarooshi 2005), they underemphasize their organizational cultures and internal politics.

International legal theories can be divided into norm-based models and interest-based models (Hathaway 2005; Hathaway and Koh 2004). Norm-based models build on constructivist questions of how norms evolve and identities are constituted. They focus on the role of principled ideas in motivating the behavior of actors, including states and IOs. They include managerial theory and the transnational legal process school, which have focused on the question of why states comply with international norms (see Chayes and Chayes 1995; Koh 1997). Scholars have also measured the extent of countries' implementation and compliance with treaties over time (see Weiss and Jacobson 1998). In addition, there is a growing literature on mechanisms of norm socialization to explain how law influences state behavior (see, e.g., Goodman and Jinks 2004). Yet this scholarship has not investigated the process of norm development within IOs. What is needed is evidence of what David Kennedy calls "the vocabularies, expertise, and sensibility of the professionals who manage . . . background norms and institutions, [which] are central elements in global governance" (2005, 7). As my study of the Bank affirms, the actions and decisions of bureaucrats are critical factors that shape how international institutions operate and influence state behavior.

Interest-based models present a rationalist account to explain state interests and behavior (see, e.g., Goldsmith and Posner 2005). This approach challenges normative models by viewing international legal obligations in purely instrumental terms. According to these theories, international law, as well as the behavior of IOs, can be understood by examining states, which act rationally to maximize their interests (ibid.). I contend, however, that state interests alone cannot explain or predict how international institutions behave. In the cases where member state interests compete and diverge from the interests of officials within the organizations, then IOs can act as autonomous agents.

My study demonstrates that institutions can have relative autonomy when member states hold competing preferences and do not reach consensus. In these circumstances, IO officials have discretion and can significantly influence how the institution behaves. IOs vary with respect to the amount of autonomy they have with respect to member states (see Hawkins et al. 2006). Though some have limited discretion to stray from state interests, others like the Bank have broad discretion when member states disagree. The Bank's member states cast a shadow over the Bank, but what has been underemphasized is how much autonomy the agency has in pushing issues forward under the radar. By conducting ethnographic research on the Bank, I was able to uncover the formal and informal norms and the decision-making processes within the institution that shape state behavior.

This study also reveals the competing subcultures and other internal contestations that may impede norm internalization. Why are certain norms and policies adopted in an institution while others are not? Analysis of organizational culture can explain how and why certain norms are framed, interpreted, and implemented by IO officials. IR scholars describe a case of unsuccessful norm diffusion as "the dog that didn't bark" (Checkel 1999, 86). The case of the diffusion of human rights at the World Bank is more precisely a case of the "dog that didn't bark—at least initially." My research uncovers why human rights norms have been historically rejected by the Bank and only recently moved closer to being adopted and internalized. It is important to study these cases to identity the conditions of possibility for the internalization of norms within IOs.

By analyzing the early success of the recent initiative to economize human rights, this study suggests the limits of human rights legalization in particular institutional contexts. Internal advocates have learned from previous failed attempts to mainstream the agenda and realized that the degree of "legalization" of human rights norms has influenced whether Bank staff adopt and internalize them. My study departs from conventional writing on legalization with regard to definition and strategic value for implementing human rights. When legal scholars discuss *legalization*, they often refer to the following definition used in recent literature in international relations (IR): as "a particular form of institutionalization characterized by three components: obligation, precision, and delegation" (Abbott et al. 2000, 401; see also Goldstein et al. 2001). According to this definition, legalization describes "a particular set of characteristics that institutions may (or may not) possess" (Abbott et al. 2000, 401). This conception is more applicable to an institutional regime or arrangement (e.g., European Community law or WTO agreements) than to the structure or status of a specific norm within an institution. By studying institutions only as the subjects of legalization, IR scholars do not acknowledge the organic nature of legalization and the process by which it occurs and may be contested *within* institutions.

I focus here on a different aspect of legalization: the extent to which norms are perceived as having legal status, often in relation to an existing legal system (e.g., the international human rights regime). In other words, to what degree are norms conceived as "legal" norms (rather than moral, cultural, or professional norms, for instance)? This understanding of legalization addresses the relationship between a norm and its legal expression, and whether "legal norms, as a type, operate differently from any other kind of norms" (Finnemore 2000, 701). With respect to human rights, these norms could be framed as moral or political concepts, as well as legal concepts. Amartya Sen has critiqued "the entirely law-dependent views of human rights" and argued that they be defined as ethical rather than legal claims (2006, 2916–17). He believes that "human rights can have influence without necessarily depending on coercive legal rules" (2006, 2921; see also Sen 2004). Going one step further, there are instances when a law-dependent view of human rights can hinder its influence.

This leads us to an assessment of the strategic value of human rights legalization (see Donnelly 2006). In the past few decades, there has been a trend toward the legalization of human rights and international institutions in general (Jinks 2002). Legal scholars have emphasized the benefits of legalization, which "tends to bolster the credibility of normative commitments, increase compliance with international norms, and provide a highly rationalized mode of clarifying and resolving interpretive disagreements" (361). Yet there are costs associated with human rights legalization, particularly when it occurs in institutional environments that value nonlegal principles or seek nonlegal goals (such as respect for moral values like dignity). For example, during the creation of human rights commissions in postauthoritarian regimes in the 1990s, there were attempts "to detach human rights from their legal moorings and redefine them as a generalized language of public morality" (Wilson 2006a, 84). Citing the harmful consequences of overlegalization, Laurence Helfer advocated for a cost-benefit view of legalization in his case study (2002) of the Caribbean backlash against human rights regimes. Although Helfer adopted the IR definition of legalization and applied it to human rights treaties rather than norms within institutions, he raised important questions about the usefulness of legalization in particular contexts. Helfer's study suggests that the legalization of international human rights norms does not necessarily increase state compliance with those norms. In the case of three Commonwealth Caribbean countries, the governments withdrew from international human rights treaties as a reaction to the Privy Council's (the region's highest appellate court) overlegalization of treaty obligations regarding supranational review of death row petitions.

In examining why legal norms could have distinctive effects in certain institutional contexts but not others, Martha Finnemore noted that "an organization staffed mostly by lawyers is likely to find legal norms more persuasive than other kinds of norms and to give them special weight. . . . If economists (or members of some other profession) dominated policy making, we would expect norms of that profession, and not legal norms, to be particularly powerful" (2000, 701). Finnemore's example applies aptly to the case of the World Bank.

My research demonstrates that legalizing human rights has not been an effective strategy for their adoption at the Bank. Overemphasizing the legal dimension of human rights norms has limited their persuasiveness and impeded their internalization. According to some Bank officials, human rights law invokes the political dimension of human rights by critiquing state behavior on the basis of binding standards that are left open to political manipulation, and serving as a trump that overrides all other concerns, including economic efficiency. As David Kinley observed:

> It appears to be the combination of the moral force of human rights *qua* rights and the fact of their encasement within international law that is particularly troubling for economists and Bank officials alike. Thus arises the desire to uncouple the two dimensions and instead treat human rights as "high priority goals" (accepting their moral force), rather than legally binding obligations [Kinley 2006, 368, citing Gauri 2003].

As a result, internal advocates have begun depoliticizing human rights by framing them for economists and underscoring their instrumental value. This strategy is an attempt to minimize their obligatory force, nonnegotiable structure, and trumping power. By doing so, human rights lose their emancipatory potential to make claims that may upset the institution's dominant ideology.

Unpacking International Institutions

By analyzing the culture of an international economic institution through the lens of human rights, this study uncovers how bureaucratic experts negotiate the competing values that underlie global governance. Additional ethnographic studies of global institutions would further illuminate how international law and norms are produced, contested, and translated. It is important to analyze the internal dynamics within these institutions, including the making of policy, the movement of ideas, and the production and circulation of knowledge. My study particularly has focused on the internal conflicts between employees over incorporation and translation of human rights norms. It uncovered how multiple normative frameworks can compete within an institution. Interpretive gaps between these frameworks may lead to underimplementation or inconsistent compliance to norms, whether human rights or otherwise.

Unpacking international institutions means studying power dynamics and interactions not only between bureaucrats but also among the variety of actors who interact with them, such as civil society advocates. If I were to extend my study of the Bank, I would examine the relationship between employees in the headquarters and those in field offices. Anecdotal evidence suggests that employees in the field offices are less influenced by power politics between departments than by the domestic politics in the countries where they are situated. A further extension of my project would be to study employees within the subagencies of the Bank, including the International Finance Corporation (IFC) and the Multilateral Investment Guarantee Agency. My interviews with several IFC employees revealed that the IFC's organizational culture is quite distinct from that of the Bank. This is true for a number of reasons: (1) the IFC's clients are distinct from those of the Bank (companies rather than countries); (2) the IFC is dominated not by economists but by business professionals with MBAs, so the disciplinary divisions differ from those within the Bank; (3) the IFC's work is more project-focused, with few resources spent on research papers (since there are no "network" advisory units as there are in the Bank); and (4) the IFC is subject to pressure not only from civil society activists but also from corporations that have looked to the IFC for guidance on enhancing social and environmental sustainability in investment projects. Although I conducted limited research on the IFC, my preliminary findings suggest the need for more comprehensive study of subagencies that may operate quite independently from their parent institution.

Another element of international institutions that is worthy of further study is the role of their governing boards and member states. I did not focus my research at the Bank on its board, but my select interviews with executive directors and their staff revealed the level of discretion that employees exercise in ways that depart from the interests of member states (i.e., under the radar of the board). What remains unclear is which issues they have the most discretion over, and the extent to which executive directors are aware of employee behavior in this regard and nonetheless silently condone it. Moreover, it would be useful to study the professional background of executive directors and their staff. If board staff are appointed from their countries' ministries of finance, this would suggest that their conceptions of human rights and other issues closely resemble those of Bank economists. Is there a clash of expertise within the board as there is within the Bank? These issues require that we open the black box of the Board of Executive Directors, and similar governing boards of international institutions, in the same way that this study aimed to do so with regard to the Bank's bureaucracy.

Scholarship that unpacks international institutions can inform strategies for how to frame norms to effectively facilitate their internalization. Advocates need to recognize that organizations require appropriately tailored human rights campaigns corresponding to their distinct mandates, management structures, informal and formal incentive systems, and decision-making processes. Numerous existing strategies are based on law since many advocates are largely resistant to straying from a legal framework for fear that an alternative framework would dilute the human rights principles. My research demonstrates that this commitment to legalizing human rights hindered progress in pushing the agenda forward in economic-oriented organizations like the World Bank. On a broader level, I hope my ethnography can inspire advocates and policy makers to take into account the internal conflicts within institutions that may impede effective policy implementation.

Notes

Introduction

1. The term *World Bank Group* encompasses all five institutions, including the International Finance Corporation, the Multilateral Investment Guarantee Agency, and the International Centre for Settlement of Investment Disputes. The term *World Bank*, as I use it here, refers specifically to two of the five, the International Bank for Reconstruction and Development (IBRD) and the International Development Association (IDA).

2. There are minor exceptions, which I discuss in Chapter 4. For instance, some Bank documents have referred to human rights, and some employees indirectly work on certain human rights, particularly economic, social, and cultural rights.

3. The World Bank normally develops a Country Assistance Strategy every one to three years in consultation with the borrower country's government and civil society organizations. This strategy addresses the country's top development priorities, creditworthiness, and past portfolio performance, as well as the level of financial and technical assistance that the Bank seeks to give the country.

4. For an analysis of the relationship between human rights in theory and practice, see Cowan, Dembour, and Wilson 2001.

5. The World Bank Inspection Panel is a quasi-independent forum created in 1993 for local citizens to file complaints against the Bank for failure to follow its own policies.

Chapter 1

1. A prominent example of this framework is the Voluntary Principles on Security and Human Rights, which promotes human rights risk assessments in the extractive industries sector. Voluntary Principles on Security and Human Rights, available at http://www.voluntaryprinciples.org (last accessed on Dec. 5, 2011).

2. See, e.g., Herz et al. (2008), representing views from several NGOs, including the Center for International Environmental Law, Bank Information Center, Oxfam Australia, and World Resources Institute.

3. The UN Global Compact aims to encourage companies to embrace nine principles drawn from the Universal Declaration of Human Rights, the International Labor Organization's Fundamental Principles on Rights at Work, and the Rio Principles on Environment and Development. In addition to individual companies and international business associations, the Global Compact participants include the UN (the Secretary General's Office, Office of the High Commissioner for Human Rights, International Labor Organization, UN Environment Programme, and the UNDP), the International Confederation of Free Trade Unions, and more than a dozen NGOs. See http://www.globalcompact.org (last accessed on Dec. 5, 2011).

4. International Finance Corporation, "IFC Safeguards Update: Discussion on Human Rights," Summary Notes (Feb. 14, 2005).

5. The "Equator Principles": A Financial Industry Benchmark for Determining, Assessing and Managing Social and Environmental Risk in Project Financing, at preamble (2003), www.equator-principles.com/resources/equator-principles.pdf (last accessed on Dec. 5, 2011).

6. Interview with official, Human Rights Watch, Washington, DC (July 20, 2006).

7. See, e.g., *Doe et al. v. Unocal Corporation et al.*, 110 F.Supp.2d 1294 (C.D. Cal. 2000).

8. Sub-Commission on the Promotion and Protection of Human Rights, Norms on the Responsibilities of Transnational Corporations and Other Business Enterprises with Regard to Human Rights, UN Doc. E/CN.4/Sub.2/2003/12/Rev.2 (2003), http://www.unhchr.ch/huridocda/huridoca.nsf/%28Symbol%29/E.CN.4.Sub.2.2003.12.Rev.2.En (last accessed on Dec. 5, 2011).

9. John Ruggie, Special Representative of the UN Secretary-General, Guiding Principles on Business and Human Rights: Implementing the United Nations "Protect, Respect and Remedy" Framework, UN Doc. A/HRC/17/31 (2011).

10. Interview with official, Environment and Social Development Department, International Finance Corporation, Washington, DC (May 9, 2006).

11. Interview with official, Bank Information Center, Washington, DC (Jan. 31, 2006).

12. Interview with official, Human Rights Watch, Washington, DC (July 20, 2006).

13. Interview with official, Bank Information Center, Washington, DC (Jan. 31, 2006).

14. Ibid. See Articles of Agreement of the International Bank for Reconstruction and Development, Art. IV, sec. 10, July 22, 1944, 60 Stat. 1440 (1945), 2 U.N.T.S. 134 (1947) [hereinafter Articles of Agreement].

15. Interview with official, Poverty Reduction and Economic Management Department, Africa Region, World Bank, Washington, DC (May 17, 2006).

16. Ibid.

17. Interview with James Wolfensohn, former president, World Bank, New York (June 14, 2007).

18. "Human Rights and Sustainable Development: What Role for the Bank?" summary of proceedings, p. 10 (May 2, 2002).

19. Ibid. at 12.

20. Ibid. at 11.

21. Under an overarching goal of "the promotion of social development of all the world's peoples," the set of principles in *Principles and Good Practice in Social Policy* fall within four areas: achieving universal access to basic social services; enabling all men and women to attain secure, sustainable livelihoods and decent working conditions; promoting systems of social protection; and fostering social integration (World Bank 1999, 2).

22. Interview with former official, Social Development Department, World Bank, Washington, DC (Feb. 16, 2006).

23. "Human Rights and Sustainable Development: What Role for the Bank?" summary of proceedings, pp. 6 7 (May 2, 2002). At the 2002 meeting, Sfeir-Younis asserted, "Economic policies without regard for human rights are inappropriate and incomplete, and a human rights package without economics is, at worst, simply a false promise or, at best, an act that will yield only short term benefits." Ibid. at 7.

24. Interview with former official, Social Development Department, World Bank, Washington, DC (Feb. 16, 2006).

25. Ibid.

26. The task force didn't seek to bring the issue to the full Board of Executive Directors but only its Development Committee, since it did not want to sharpen existing divisions on the board. Members of the task force now regret they didn't at least prepare a public statement based on their work.

27. Interview with former official, Social Development Department, World Bank, Washington, DC (Feb. 16, 2006).

28. The Bank's managing directors rank directly below the president.

29. Interview with official, External Affairs Department, World Bank, Washington, DC (Mar. 15, 2006).

30. I met this lawyer when I interned at the Bank in the summer of 2002, and she later approached me to coauthor a report with her on human rights in ECA.

31. Interview with official, Bank Information Center, Washington, DC (Jan. 31, 2006).

32. Interview with James Wolfensohn, former president, World Bank, New York (June 14, 2007).

33. Interview with official, Human Rights Watch, Washington, DC (July 20, 2006).

34. Interview with official, External Affairs Department, World Bank, Washington, DC (Mar. 15, 2006).

35. One employee described her as being "pitchforked" into her position from outside the Bank, rather than rising from within the ranks. As a result, she did not understand the Bank's language well and had trouble carrying out her mandate effectively. Interview with official, Development Research Group, World Bank, Wash-

ington, DC (Feb. 14, 2006). In contrast, another managing director, Shengman Zhang, commanded more respect at the Bank because he had worked at the institution for a long time and all of the operational vice presidents reported to him. Interview with official, External Affairs Department, World Bank, Washington, DC (Mar. 15, 2006).

36. Interview with official, Human Development Network, World Bank, Washington, DC (Jan. 24, 2006).

37. Interview with official, Legal Department, World Bank, Washington, DC (Jan. 4, 2006).

38. Interview with official, Legal Department, World Bank, Washington, DC (Feb. 21, 2006).

39. Interview with representative from an international organization for trade unions, Washington, DC (Feb. 14, 2006).

40. Interview with official, Human Development Network, World Bank, Washington, DC (Jan. 24, 2006).

Chapter 2

1. Interview with James Wolfensohn, former president, World Bank, New York (June 14, 2007).

2. Ibid.

3. Ibid.

4. Interview with representative from an international organization for trade unions, Washington, DC (Feb. 14, 2006).

5. See "Interpretation of the Agreement of 25 March 1951 Between the WHO and Egypt, Advisory Opinion," Dec. 20, 1980, *International Court of Justice Report* 73, 89–90.

6. See "Reparation for Injuries Suffered in the Service of the United Nations, Advisory Opinion," Apr. 11, 1949, *International Court of Justice Report* 174.

7. See "Agreement Between the United Nations and the International Bank for Reconstruction and Development," Art. IV(2), Sept. 16 and Nov. 15, 1947, 16 UNTS 346, 348.

8. Articles of Agreement, Art. IV, sec. 10, and Art. III, sec. 5(b).

9. Dañino resigned from the Bank on January 13, 2006.

10. According to some legal scholars, Shihata's economic test is ambiguous and does not contain clear criteria. It "does not stipulate the time period over which the directness and the obviousness of the economic impact of the particular factor should be determined. If the time period for analysis is short, then relatively few nonobvious economic issues will have a direct and obvious effect" (Bradlow 1996, 61, citing Shihata 2000b, 271–72).

11. Interview with official, Legal Department, World Bank, Washington, DC (Jan. 4, 2006).

12. Kinley cites Pascal Lamy's speech, "Humanizing Globalization," in Santiago,

Chile (Jan. 30, 2006). http://www.wto.org/english/news_e/sppl_e/sppl16_e.htm (last accessed on Dec. 5, 2011).

13. Personal communication with Bank official (Feb. 1, 2006).

14. World Bank, "The World Bank Policy on Disclosure of Information," para. 75 (2002).

15. An acting general counsel took Dañino's place until April, when the next general counsel, Ana Palacio, took office.

16. Interview with official, Legal Department, World Bank, Washington, DC (May 25, 2006).

17. Interview with Roberto Dañino, former general counsel, World Bank, Washington, DC (May 26, 2006).

18. Interview with official, Legal Department, World Bank, Washington, DC (May 25, 2006).

19. Interview with official, Sustainable Development Network, World Bank, Washington, DC (Feb. 1, 2006).

20. Interview with official, Legal Department, World Bank, Washington, DC (Feb. 21, 2006).

21. Interview with official, Legal Department, World Bank, Washington, DC (May 1, 2006).

Chapter 3

1. Interview with official, Legal Department, World Bank, Washington, DC (Jan. 4, 2006).

2. Interview with official, Legal Department, World Bank, Washington, DC (Mar. 9, 2006).

3. Interview with official, Poverty Reduction and Economic Management Network, World Bank, Washington, DC (May 4, 2006).

4. Interview with official, Development Research Group, World Bank, Washington, DC (Mar. 14, 2006).

5. Interview with official, Independent Evaluation Group, World Bank, Washington, DC (Nov. 16, 2005).

6. Interview with official, Social Development Department, Latin America and the Caribbean Region, World Bank, Washington, DC (Nov. 15, 2005).

7. Interview with official, World Bank Institute, World Bank, Washington, DC (Nov. 10, 2005).

8. Interview with official, East Asia and Pacific Region, World Bank, Washington, DC (Nov. 9, 2005).

9. Ibid.

10. Ibid.

11. Interview with official, Human Resources, World Bank, Washington, DC (May 5, 2006).

12. Interview with former official, Social Development Department, Latin America and the Caribbean Region, World Bank, Washington, DC (Apr. 5, 2006).

13. Interview with official, East Asia and Pacific Region, World Bank, Washington, DC (Nov. 9, 2005).

14. Interview with official, Environment Department, Latin America and the Caribbean Region, World Bank, Washington, DC (Nov. 15, 2005).

15. Ibid.

16. Interview with official, Social Development Department, Latin America and the Caribbean Region, World Bank, Washington, DC (Mar. 15, 2006).

17. Interview with official, East Asia and Pacific Region, World Bank, Washington, DC (Nov. 9, 2005).

18. Social Development Orientation, World Bank, Washington, DC (Jan. 19, 2006).

19. Interview with official, Independent Evaluations Group, World Bank, Washington, DC (Apr. 5, 2006).

20. The World Bank, *The World Bank Operational Manual*, Table A1, OP 4.00 (July 2005), "Environmental and Social Policies—Policy Objectives and Operational Principles."

21. In 1998, the Bank began revising Operational Directive 4.20 into a new policy, Operational Policy 4.10, which was approved in 2005.

22. Interview with former official, Social Development Department, Latin America and the Caribbean Region, World Bank, Washington, DC (Nov. 14, 2005).

23. Ibid.

24. Interview with official, Legal Department, World Bank, Washington, DC (Mar. 9, 2006).

25. Interview with official, Social Development Department, Latin America and the Caribbean Region, World Bank, Washington, DC (Mar. 15, 2006).

26. Interview with official, World Bank Institute, World Bank, Washington, DC (Nov. 10, 2005).

27. Interview with official, Sustainable Development Network, World Bank, Washington, DC (Feb. 1, 2006).

28. The Bank issued Operational Directive (OD) 4.20 in 1991. Although OD 4.20 was replaced in 2005 by OP 4.10, I focus on the earlier policy because there is more evidence of its implementation or lack of same.

29. Operations Evaluation Department, World Bank, Report No. 25,332, *Implementation of Operational Directive 4.20 on Indigenous Peoples: An Independent Desk Review*, para. 3.4 (2003) [hereinafter *OED Desk Review*]. The OED examined all 234 projects that were appraised after 1992, which was when OD 4.20 came into effect, and closed before May 2001 (para. 3.1). When determining whether the operational directive had been applied to projects, it looked for projects with an indigenous peoples development plan or with elements of an indigenous peoples plan, "namely: sound diagnosis of issues related to IP [indigenous peoples], participation of IP

in project design and implementation, measures to protect the interests of IP, and monitoring indicators for IP-related results" (para. 1.13). The OED also considered projects that lacked these elements to varying degrees but included other measures to protect indigenous peoples.

30. Ibid. para. 3.12. The OED rated projects as applying the policy in a satisfactory or highly satisfactory way if they included a sound diagnosis of issues related to indigenous peoples, participation of indigenous peoples in design and implementation, and measures to protect the interests of indigenous peoples. Projects that lacked such diagnosis of issues were rated moderately satisfactory, while those with a lower level of participation or none were rated moderately unsatisfactory or unsatisfactory (p. 17, table 3.3).

31. An indigenous peoples development plan includes an assessment of the country's legal framework as it relates to indigenous peoples, baseline data including up-to-date maps and analysis of the peoples' social structure and production activities, assistance with the country's recognition of traditional land tenure systems, and a strategy for local participation. Although the indigenous peoples development plan is the borrower country's responsibility under OD 4.20, preparation, appraisal, implementation, and supervision of the plan require significant involvement and technical assistance by Bank staff.

32. OED Desk Review, supra note 29, para. 4.8.

33. Ibid., p. 26, box 4.2.

34. Interview with official, Social Development Department, Latin America and the Caribbean Region, World Bank, Washington, DC (Nov. 15, 2005).

35. Portfolio Management Task Force, World Bank, "Effective Implementation: Key to Development Impact" (Discussion Draft 1992, hereinafter Wapenhans Report).

36. The decreasing portfolio quality was measured according to the Bank's own performance criteria, including a minimum 10 percent rate of return. The most common performance problems were "institutional constraints including [b]orrower inertia, shortages of counterpart financing resulting from deterioration in the macro environment, poor project management and defective procurement." In those projects with performance problems, the time required for completion often exceeded the time estimated at appraisal, and borrowers' compliance with legal covenants was low (Wapenhans Report 1992, iii, 3).

37. See Wolfensohn's 1996 address to the Bank/Fund annual meetings in Washington, DC.

38. There are many critics of the Bank's research, including those who feel the Bank is too tied to its own paradigms. An independent evaluation of the Bank's research, by top academic economists, criticized it for being "used to proselytize on behalf of Bank policy, often without taking a balanced view of the evidence, and without expressing appropriate skepticism" (Banerjee et al. 2006).

39. As of July 1, 2006, the Bank merged a number of thematic areas, resulting in a reduction from seven to five. The current thematic areas are Financial and Private

Sector Development, Human Development, Operations Policy and Country Services, Poverty Reduction and Economic Management, and Sustainable Development.

40. My description is based on a 2004 new staff orientation PowerPoint presentation "The Matrix Environment and the World Bank."

41. Interview with official, Legal Department, World Bank, Washington, DC (Dec. 8, 2005).

42. Interview with official, Environment Department, Latin America and the Caribbean Region, World Bank, Washington, DC (Nov. 15, 2005).

43. The 2002 estimate takes into account both staff and short-term consultants. It includes 175 social development specialists, 22 gender specialists, and 249 additional Bank staff members who hold graduate degrees in the non-economic social sciences.

44. Interview with former official, Social Development Department, Latin America and the Caribbean Region, World Bank, Washington, DC (Apr. 5, 2006).

45. Interview with official, Legal Department, World Bank, Washington, DC (May 1, 2006).

46. Interview with former official, World Bank, Washington, DC (May 15, 2006).

47. The cancellation of Nepal's Arun III Hydroelectric Dam was in part due to "the *reciprocal interaction* between external critics and . . . insider advocates of environmental and social concerns within the Bank" (Fox and Brown 1998, 1, 4). Although a number of factors generally contribute to the Bank's cancellation of a loan, an alliance between civil society critics and internal Bank dissidents can play an important role.

48. Interview with official, Development Research Group, World Bank, Washington, DC (Feb. 14, 2006).

49. One exception is the Young Professionals Program, which recruits twenty to forty talented young people from a variety of professional backgrounds, including economics.

50. On the rare occasions that operations staff do have time to write, their audience is usually development practitioners rather than academics.

51. Interview with official, Development Research Group, World Bank, Washington, DC (Feb. 14, 2006).

52. In 2004, Dañino tried to raise the prestige of the Legal Department by establishing the Legal Associates Program, which recruits talented young lawyers from around the world for a two-year stint in the department and possibly permanent employment thereafter. His motivation was to inspire a new generation of lawyers to join the Bank.

53. Interview with official, Legal Department, World Bank, Washington, DC (Dec. 8, 2005).

54. Interview with official, Legal Department, World Bank, Washington, DC (Jan. 4, 2006).

55. Interview with official, Development Research Group, World Bank, Washington, DC (Feb. 14, 2006).

56. The shifting status of the Bank's Legal Department is not unusual among international organizations. For instance, the Legal Department of the International Monetary Fund (IMF) played an influential role in the institution under General Counsel Joseph Gold from 1960 to 1979. Following Gold's retirement, however, the position of "General Counsel and Director of the Legal Department" was downgraded to just "Director of the Legal Department," which reflected "a denigration of law within the IMF." Legal considerations played a less significant role in IMF decision making after Gold's tenure, although they returned to prominence in the late 1980s when the title of "General Counsel" was again added to the "Director of the Legal Department" position. The changing title of the head of the Legal Department indicates the shifting status of lawyers within the organization (Edwards 2008).

57. The Bank's Articles of Agreement state: "Subject to the general control of the Executive Directors, [the president] shall be responsible for the organization, appointment and dismissal of the officers and staff." Articles of Agreement, Art. V, Section 5.

58. Shihata notes that "the role of the [general counsel], and that of Bank lawyers generally, has evolved with the evolution of the role of the Bank itself" (1997, 221).

59. Informal interview with officials, World Bank, Washington, DC (July 26, 2006).

60. Personal communication with official, Legal Department, World Bank, Washington, DC (Feb. 2, 2006).

Chapter 4

1. Interview with official, Independent Evaluation Group, World Bank, Washington, DC (Nov. 16, 2005).

2. Interview with official, Legal Department, World Bank, Washington, DC (Jan. 17, 2006).

3. Interview with official, Social Development Department, Latin America and the Caribbean Region, World Bank, Washington, DC (Nov. 15, 2005).

4. Interview with former official, World Bank, Washington, DC (May 15, 2006).

5. Ibid.

6. Interview with official, Legal Department, World Bank, Washington, DC (May 25, 2006).

7. Interview with official, Legal Department, World Bank, Washington, DC (May 1, 2006).

8. Ibid.

9. The World Bank, *The World Bank Operational Manual*, OP 4.10 (July 2005), "Indigenous Peoples."

10. Interview with official, Latin America and the Caribbean Region, World Bank, Washington, DC (May 23, 2006).

11. Interview with official, Independent Evaluation Group, World Bank, Washington, DC (Nov. 16, 2005).

12. Interview with official, World Bank Institute, World Bank, Washington, DC (Nov. 10, 2005).

13. Interview with official, Independent Evaluation Group, World Bank, Washington, DC (Nov. 16, 2005).

14. The capability approach is a theoretical framework developed by Amartya Sen for understanding poverty and human development. It is based on the freedom to achieve well-being as understood in terms of people's functional capabilities. According to Sen, human rights is a much broader (and in some ways more appropriate) framework since it includes due process rights such as fair treatment that are not capabilities. (Interview with Amartya Sen, Thomas W. Lamont University Professor and professor of economics and philosophy, Harvard University, Cambridge, Massachusetts (May 23, 2006)). See also Sen 2004, 336.

15. Interview with official, Independent Evaluation Group, World Bank, Washington, DC (Nov. 16, 2005).

16. Interview with official, Latin America and the Caribbean Region, World Bank, Washington, DC (May 23, 2006).

17. Interview with official, Legal Department, World Bank, Washington, DC (Jan. 17, 2006).

18. Interview with official, Legal Department, World Bank, Washington, DC (May 1, 2006).

19. Ibid.

20. Universal Declaration of Human Rights, GA Res. 217A, UN GAOR, 3d Sess., Resolutions, at 71, UN Doc. A/810 (1948).

21. Interviews with officials, Legal Department, World Bank, Washington, DC (Jan. 4 and Jan. 17, 2006).

22. Interview with former official, Social Development Department, World Bank, Washington, DC (Feb. 16, 2006).

23. This goal explicitly follows from the commitments agreed on at the March 1995 World Summit for Social Development in Copenhagen.

24. See http://www.ifc.org/PerformanceStandards (last accessed on Mar. 8, 2012).

25. See the Universal Declaration of Human Rights (Art. 25 (1)); the International Covenant on Economic, Social and Cultural Rights (Art. 12); the Convention on the Rights of the Child (Art. 24); and the Convention on the Elimination of All Forms of Discrimination against Women (Art. 12).

26. "International Guidelines on HIV/AIDS and Human Rights," UNCHR res. 1997/33, U.N. Doc. E/CN.4/1997/150 (1997).

27. World Bank, "Project Appraisal Document on a Proposed Loan to St. Lucia for HIV/AIDS Prevention and Control Project," Report No. 29129 (June 1, 2004).

28. Ibid., p. 5.

29. Ibid., pp. 2–3.

30. Ibid., p. 9.

31. World Bank, "Project Appraisal Document on a Proposed Loan to the Rus-

sian Federation for a Tuberculosis and AIDS Control Project," Report No. 21239-RU (Mar. 10, 2003).

32. Ibid., p. 2.

33. Ibid.

34. Then-President Wolfensohn had approached the Nordic countries in 2004 and asked for their assistance in advancing a human rights agenda at the Bank. It took about two years to make the arrangements to bring in the senior lawyer from the Danish Ministry of Foreign Affairs. It is not uncommon for countries to fund appointment of a Bank staff member to pursue a particular policy agenda.

35. "The World Bank and Human Rights: Nordic-Baltic Working Paper" (Oct. 20, 2005).

36. Ibid.

37. "Justice and Human Rights Trust Fund Concept Note" (July 12, 2006).

38. See "The Nordic Trust Fund" at the Bank's website, http://go.worldbank.org/PKPTI6FU40 (last accessed on Dec. 5, 2011).

39. Daniel Kaufmann, statement, in *Conference on the Establishment of a Justice and Human Rights Trust Fund (JHRTF) in the World Bank*, Proceedings (Copenhagen, June 26–27, 2006), p. 11.

40. Interview with official, Development Research Group, World Bank, Washington, DC (Mar. 14, 2006).

41. World Bank Legal Department, "The Proposed Nordic Trust Fund & Emerging Human Rights Practice in the Bank" (Mar. 2006; emphasis removed).

42. Participants at the workshop included about thirty representatives from the World Bank, the Nordic-Baltic Foreign Ministries, and academic experts in human rights from four continents.

43. Interview with official, External Affairs Department, World Bank, Washington, DC (Mar. 13, 2006).

44. Interview with former official, Social Development Department, Latin America and the Caribbean Region, World Bank, Washington, DC (April 5, 2006).

45. "Stockholm Seminar on Human Rights Dialogues and Rights Principles in Development Cooperation at the Country-Level," Summary of Discussions (June 19–20, 2006).

46. Joseph K. Ingram (then-World Bank special representative to the United Nations and the World Trade Organization), statement, *First Session of the Human Rights Council in Geneva Switzerland* (June 21, 2006).

47. Interview with official, Social Development Department, World Bank, Washington, DC (Mar. 15, 2006).

48. The World Bank, *The World Bank Operational Manual*, OP 4.01 (Feb. 2011), "Environmental Assessment."

49. Interview with official, Board of Executive Directors, World Bank, Washington, DC (July 24, 2006).

50. *Proceedings of the Conference on the Establishment of a Justice and Human Rights Trust Fund (JHRTF) in the World Bank,* Copenhagen, June 26–27, 2006, p. 8.

51. Interview with official, Legal Department, World Bank, Washington, DC (May 25, 2006).

Chapter 5

1. For a discussion of privatization's possible erosion of public law values, see Dickinson 2006.

Bibliography

Abbott, Andrew. 1988. *The System of Professions: An Essay on the Division of Expert Labor.* Chicago: University of Chicago Press.

Abbott, Kenneth W., Robert O. Keohane, Andrew Moravcsik, Anne-Marie Slaughter, and Duncan Snidal. 2000. "The Concept of Legalization." *International Organization* 54:401–19.

Alston, Philip, and Mary Robinson, eds. 2005. *Human Rights and Development: Towards Mutual Reinforcement.* New York: Oxford University Press.

Alvarez, José E. 2005. *International Organizations as Law-Makers.* New York: Oxford University Press.

Anders, Gerhard. 2005. "Good Governance as Technology: Towards an Ethnography of the Bretton Woods Institutions." In *The Aid Effect: Giving and Governing in International Development,* edited by David Mosse and David Lewis, 37–60. London: Pluto Press.

An-Na'im, Abdullahi Ahmed. 1992. *Human Rights in Cross-Cultural Perspectives: A Quest for Consensus.* Philadelphia: University of Pennsylvania Press.

Banerjee, Abhijit, Angus Deaton, Nora Lustig, and Ken Rogoff. 2006. *An Evaluation of World Bank Research, 1998–2005.* Washington, DC: World Bank.

Barnett, Michael N., and Martha Finnemore. 1999. "The Politics, Power, and Pathologies of International Organizations." *International Organization* 53:699–732.

———. 2004. *Rules for the World: International Organizations in Global Politics.* Ithaca, NY: Cornell University Press.

Bartlett, Christopher A., and Sumantra Ghoshal. 1990. "Matrix Management: Not a Structure, a Frame of Mind." *Harvard Business Review* 68:138–45.

Batteau, Allen. 2001. "Negations and Ambiguities in the Cultures of Organization." *American Anthropologist* 102:726–40.

Baxi, Upendra. 2002. *The Future of Human Rights.* Oxford: Oxford University Press.

Bebbington, Anthony, Scott Guggenheim, Elizabeth Olson, and Michael Woolcock.

2004. "Exploring Social Capital Debates at the World Bank." *Journal of Development Studies* 40:33–64.

Beckmann, David, Ramgopal Agarwala, Sven Burmester, and Ismail Serageldin. 1991. *Friday Morning Reflections at the World Bank: Essays on Values and Development.* Washington, DC: Seven Locks Press.

Benford, Robert D., and David A. Snow. 2000. "Framing Processes and Social Movements: An Overview and Assessment." *Annual Review of Sociology* 26:611–39.

Black, Julia. 2001. "Proceduralizing Regulation: Part II." *Oxford Journal of Legal Studies* 21:33–58.

Boisson de Chazournes, Laurence. 2000. "Policy Guidance and Compliance: The World Bank Operational Standards." In *Commitment and Compliance: The Role of Non-Binding Norms in the International Legal System,* edited by Dinah Shelton, 281–303. New York: Oxford University Press.

Bourdieu, Pierre. 1987. *Language and Symbolic Power.* Cambridge, MA: Harvard University Press.

———. 1990. *In Other Words: Essays Toward a Reflexive Sociology.* Palo Alto, CA: Stanford University Press.

Bradlow, Daniel D. 1994. "International Organizations and Private Complaints: The Case of the World Bank Inspection Panel." *Virginia Journal of International Law* 34:553–613.

———. 1996. "The World Bank, the IMF, and Human Rights." *Transnational Law and Contemporary Problems* 6:47–90.

———. 2002. "Should the International Financial Institutions Play a Role in the Implementation and Enforcement of International Humanitarian Law?" *University of Kansas Law Review* 50:695–729.

Branco, Manuel Couret. 2009. *Economics Versus Human Rights.* New York: Routledge.

Brenneis, Don. 1994. "Discourse and Discipline at the National Research Council: A Bureaucratic Bildungsroman." *Cultural Anthropology* 9:23–36.

Bretton Woods Project. 1997. "The World Bank and the State: A Recipe for Change?" http://www.brettonwoodsproject.org/art-16242 (last accessed Dec. 6, 2011).

Breyer, Stephen. 1993. *Breaking the Vicious Circle: Toward Effective Risk Regulation.* Cambridge, MA: Harvard University Press.

Campbell, Robert L. 2005. "Where Do We Stand? Common Mechanisms in Organizations and Social Movements Research." In *Social Movements and Organization Theory,* edited by Gerald F. Davis et al., 41–68. New York: Cambridge University Press.

Carothers, Thomas, ed. 2006. *Promoting the Rule of Law Abroad: In Search of Knowledge.* Washington, DC: Carnegie Endowment for International Peace.

Caufield, Catherine. 1996. *Masters of Illusion: The World Bank and the Poverty of Nations.* London: Macmillan.

Cernea, Michael M. 1996. *Social Organization and Development Anthropology: The 1995 Malinowski Award Lecture.* Environmentally Sustainable Development Studies and Monographs Series, No. 6. Washington, DC: World Bank.

Chayes, Abram, and Antonia Handler Chayes. 1995. *The New Sovereignty: Compliance with International Regulatory Agreements.* Cambridge, MA: Harvard University Press.

Checkel, Jeffrey T. 1999. "Norms, Institutions, and National Identity in Contemporary Europe." *International Studies Quarterly* 43:83–114.

Clarke, Kamari. 2009. *Fictions of Justice: The International Criminal Court and the Challenge of Legal Pluralism in Sub-Saharan Africa.* New York: Cambridge University Press.

Comaroff, Jean, and John L. Comaroff. 1991. *Of Revelation and Revolution: Christianity, Colonialism, and Consciousness in South Africa.* Chicago: University of Chicago Press.

———. 2000. "Millennial Capitalism: First Thoughts on a Second Coming." *Public Culture* 12:291–343.

———. 2004. "Criminal Obsessions, After Foucault: Postcoloniality, Policing, and the Metaphysics of Disorder." *Critical Inquiry* 30:800–824.

———. 2006. "Figuring Crime: Quantifacts and the Production of the Un/Real." *Public Culture* 18:209–46.

Comaroff, John L., and Jean Comaroff. 2006. "Law and Disorder in the Postcolony: An Introduction." In *Law and Disorder in the Postcolony,* edited by Jean Comaroff and John L. Comaroff, 1–56. Chicago: University of Chicago Press.

Cowan, Jane, Marie-Bénédicte Dembour, and Richard A. Wilson, eds. 2001. *Culture and Rights: Anthropological Perspectives.* New York: Cambridge University Press.

Danaher, Kevin, ed. 1994. *Fifty Years Is Enough: The Case Against the World Bank and the International Monetary Fund.* Boston: South End Press.

Dañino, Roberto. 2005. "The Legal Aspects of the World Bank's Work on Human Rights." In *Human Rights and Development: Towards Mutual Reinforcement,* edited by Philip Alston and Mary Robinson, 509–25. New York: Oxford University Press.

———. 2006. "Legal Opinion on Human Rights and the Work of the World Bank." (No longer available online; opinion document on file with author.)

Darrow, Mac. 2003. *Between Light and Shadow: The World Bank, the International Monetary Fund and International Human Rights Law.* Oxford: Hart.

Davenport, Thomas H. 1998. *Working Knowledge: How Organizations Manage What They Know*. Boston: Harvard Business School Press.

Davis, Gerald F., Doug McAdam, W. Richard Scott, and Mayer N. Zald, eds. 2005. *Social Movements and Organization Theory*. New York: Cambridge University Press.

Davis, Gloria. 2004. *A History of the Social Development Network in the World Bank, 1973–2002*. World Bank Social Development Working Paper No. 56. Washington, DC: World Bank.

Deal, Terrence E., and Allan A. Kennedy. 1982. *Corporate Cultures: The Rites and Rituals of Corporate Life*. Harmondsworth: Penguin.

Decker, Klaus, Siobhán McInerney-Lankford, and Caroline Sage. 2005. "Human Rights and Equitable Development: 'Ideals,' Issues, and Implications." Background paper for World Bank 2006.

Dezalay, Yves, and Bryant Garth. 2002. *The Internationalization of Palace Wars: Lawyers, Economists and the Transformation of Latin-American States*. Chicago: University of Chicago Press.

Dickinson, Laura A. 2006. "Public Law Values in a Privatized World." *Yale Journal of International Law* 31:383–426.

Donnelly, Jack. 2006. "The Virtues of Legalization." In *The Legalization of Human Rights: Multidisciplinary Perspectives on Human Rights and Human Rights Law*, edited by Saladin Meckled-García and Basak Çali, 67–79. Abingdon, UK: Routledge.

Douglas, Mary. 1966. *Purity and Danger: An Analysis of Concepts of Pollution and Taboo*. New York: Praeger.

Dworkin, Ronald. 1977. *Taking Rights Seriously*. Cambridge, MA: Harvard University Press.

Edwards Jr., Richard W. 2008. "The Role of the General Counsel of an International Financial Institution." *Kansas Journal of Law and Public Policy* 17:254–72.

Einhorn, Jessica. 2001. "The World Bank's Mission Creep." *Foreign Affairs* 80:22–31.

Escobar, Arturo. 1995. *Encountering Development: The Making and Unmaking of the Third World*. Princeton, NJ: Princeton University Press.

Espeland, Wendy. 1997. "Authority by the Numbers: Porter on Quantification, Discretion, and the Legitimation of Expertise." *Law and Social Inquiry* 22:1107–33.

———. 1998. *The Struggle for Water: Politics, Rationality, and Identity in the American Southwest*. Chicago: University of Chicago Press.

———, and Mitchell L. Stevens. 1998. "Commensuration as a Social Process." *Annual Review of Sociology* 24:313–43.

Falk, Richard A. 2000. *Human Rights Horizons: The Pursuit of Justice in a Globalizing World*. New York: Routledge.

Ferguson, James. 1990. *The Anti-Politics Machine: Development, Depoliticization, and Bureaucratic Power in Lesotho.* New York: Cambridge University Press.

Finnemore, Martha. 2000. "Are Legal Norms Distinctive?" *International Law and Politics* 32:699–705.

Foucault, Michel. 1977. *Discipline and Punish: The Birth of the Prison.* New York: Pantheon Books.

———. 1978. *The History of Sexuality.* Vol. 1: *An Introduction.* New York: Pantheon Books.

———. 1980. *Power/Knowledge: Selected Interviews and Other Writings 1972–1977.* Edited by Colin Gordon. New York: Pantheon Books.

Fourcade, Marion. 2006. "The Construction of a Global Profession: The Transnationalization of Economics." *American Journal of Sociology* 112:145–94.

———. 2009. *Economists and Societies: Discipline and Profession in the United States, Britain, and France, 1890s to 1990s.* Princeton, NJ: Princeton University Press.

Fox, Jonathan. 2003. "Advocacy Research and the World Bank: Propositions for Discussion." *Development in Practice* 13:519–27.

———, and L. David Brown. 1998. "Introduction." In *The Struggle for Accountability: The World Bank, NGOs, and Grassroots Movements,* edited by Jonathan A. Fox and L. David Brown, 1–47. Cambridge, MA: MIT Press.

Fukuda-Parr, Sakiko. 2003. "The Human Development Paradigm: Operationalizing Sen's Ideas on Capabilities." *Feminist Economics* 9:301–17.

Gauri, Varun. 2003. "Social Rights and Economics: Claims to Health Care and Education in Developing Countries." *World Development* 32:465–77.

Gilbert, Christopher, Andrew Powell, and David Vines. 1999. "Positioning the World Bank." *Economic Journal* 109:F598–F633.

Girdwood, John. 2007. "Reforming the World Bank: From Social-Liberalism to Neo-Liberalism." *Comparative Education* 43:413–31.

Gledhill, John. 2004. "Neoliberalism." In *A Companion to the Anthropology of Politics,* edited by David Nugent and Joan Vincent, 332–348. Oxford: Blackwell.

Goldman, Michael. 2005. *Imperial Nature: The World Bank and Struggles for Social Justice in the Age of Globalization.* New Haven, CT: Yale University Press.

Goldsmith, Jack L., and Eric A. Posner. 2005. *The Limits of International Law.* New York: Oxford University Press.

Goldstein, Judith L., Miles Kahler, Robert O. Keohane, and Anne-Marie Slaughter, eds. 2001. *Legalization and World Politics.* Cambridge, MA: MIT Press.

Goodale, Mark. 2007. "Introduction: Locating Rights, Envisioning Law Between the Global and the Local." In *The Practice of Human Rights: Tracking Law Between the Global and the Local,* edited by Mark Goodale and Sally Engle Merry, 1–38. Cambridge, UK: Cambridge University Press.

————, and Sally Engle Merry. 2007. *The Practice of Human Rights: Tracking Law Between the Global and the Local.* Cambridge, UK: Cambridge University Press.

Goodman, Ryan, and Derek Jinks. 2004. "How to Influence States: Socialization and International Human Rights Law." *Duke Law Journal* 54:621–703.

Gruskin, Sofia, and Daniel Tarantola. 2002. "Human Rights and HIV/AIDS." http://hivinsite.ucsf.edu/InSite?page=kb-08-01-07 (last accessed Dec. 6, 2011).

Gusterson, Hugh. 1996. *Nuclear Rites: A Weapons Laboratory at the End of the Cold War.* Berkeley: University of California Press.

Haas, Peter. 1992. "Introduction: Epistemic Communities and International Policy Coordination." *International Organization* 46:1–35.

Hacking, Ian. 1990. *The Taming of Chance.* Cambridge, UK: Cambridge University Press.

Halliday, Terence C., and Pavel Osinsky. 2006. "Globalization of Law." *Annual Review of Sociology* 32:447–70.

Harvey, David. 1989. *The Condition of Post-Modernity: An Enquiry into the Origins of Social Change.* Oxford: Basil Blackwell.

————. 2005. *A Brief History of Neoliberalism.* New York: Oxford University Press.

Hathaway, Oona A. 2005. "Between Power and Principle: An Integrated Theory of International Law." *University of Chicago Law Review* 72:469–536.

Hathaway, Oona A., and Harold Hongju Koh. 2004. *Foundations in International Law and Politics.* New York: Foundation Press.

Hawkins, Darren G., David A. Lake, Daniel L. Nielson, and Michael J. Tierney, eds. 2006. *Delegation and Agency in International Organizations.* Cambridge: Cambridge University Press.

Helfer, Laurence. 2002. "Overlegalizing Human Rights: International Relations Theory and the Commonwealth Caribbean Backlash Against Human Rights Regimes." *Columbia Law Review* 102:1832–1911.

Herz, Steve, Kristen Genovese, Kirk Herbertson, and Anne Perrault. August 2008. "The International Finance Corporation's Performance Standards and the Equator Principles: Respecting Human Rights and Remedying Violations?" www.ciel.org/Publications/IFC_Aug08/Ruggie_Submission.pdf (last accessed Dec. 6, 2011).

Holder, William E. 1997. "The International Monetary Fund: A Legal Perspective." *American Society of International Law Proceedings* 91:201–8.

Holmes, Douglas R., and George E. Marcus. 2005. "Cultures of Expertise and the Management of Globalization: Towards the Re-Functioning of Ethnography." In *Global Assemblages: Technology, Politics, and Ethics as Anthropological Problems,* edited by Aihwa Ong and Stephen J. Collier, 235–52. Oxford: Blackwell.

Howard-Grenville, Jennifer. 2006. "Inside the 'Black Box': How Organizational Culture and Subcultures Inform Interpretations and Actions on Environmental Issues." *Organization and Environment* 19:46–73.

International Business Leaders Forum, International Finance Corporation, and United Nations Global Compact. 2010. *Guide to Human Rights Impact Assessment and Management.* http://www.guidetohriam.org (last accessed on Dec. 5, 2011)

Jasanoff, Sheila. 2004. *States of Knowledge: The Co-Production of Science and the Social Order.* London: Routledge.

Jinks, Derek P. 2002. "The Legalization of World Politics and the Future of U.S. Human Rights Policy." *St. Louis Law Journal* 46:357–76.

Keck, Margaret, and Kathryn Sikkink. 1998. *Activists Beyond Borders: Advocacy Networks in International Politics.* Ithaca, NY: Cornell University Press.

Kennedy, David. 2005. "Challenging Expert Rule: The Politics of Global Governance." *Sydney Law Review* 27:5–28.

———. 2006. "The 'Rule of Law,' Political Choices, and Development Common Sense." In *The New Law and Economic Development*, edited by David Trubek and Alvaro Santos, 95–173. New York: Cambridge University Press.

Keohane, Robert O. 1984. *After Hegemony: Cooperation and Discord in the World Political Economy.* Princeton, NJ: Princeton University Press.

Kingsbury, Benedict. 1999. "Operational Policies of International Institutions as Part of the Law-Making Process: The World Bank and Indigenous Peoples." In *The Reality of International Law: Essays in Honour of Ian Brownlie*, edited by Guy S. Goodwin-Gill and Stefan Talmon, 323–42. New York: Oxford University Press.

Kinley, David. 2006. "Human Rights and the World Bank: Practice, Politics and Law." In *The World Bank Legal Review: Law, Equity, and Development*, edited by Ana Palacio, Caroline Mary Sage, and Michael Woolcock, 353–83. Netherlands: Martinus Nijhoff.

———. 2009. *Civilising Globalisation: Human Rights and the Global Economy.* Cambridge: Cambridge University Press.

Knorr-Cetina, Karin. 1999. *Epistemic Cultures: How the Sciences Make Knowledge.* Cambridge, MA: Harvard University Press.

Koh, Harold Hongju. 1997. "Why Do Nations Obey International Law?" *Yale Law Journal* 106:2599–2659.

Koskenniemi, Marti. 2010. "Human Rights Mainstreaming as a Project of Power." *Humanity* 1:47–59.

Latour, Bruno. 2010. *The Making of Law: An Ethnography of the Conseil d'Etat.* Cambridge, UK: Polity Press.

MacKay, Fergus. 2002. "Universal Rights or a Universe unto Itself? Indigenous Peoples' Human Rights and the World Bank's Draft Operational Policy 4.10 on Indigenous Peoples." *American University International Law Review* 17:527–624.

Marquette, Heather. 2004. "The Creeping Politicisation of the World Bank: The Case of Corruption." *Political Studies* 52:413–30.

Marshall, Katherine, and Marisa Van Saanen. 2007. *Development and Faith: Where Mind, Heart, and Soul Work Together.* Washington, DC: World Bank.

Masco, Joseph. 2006. *The Nuclear Borderlands: The Manhattan Project in Post-Cold War New Mexico.* Princeton, NJ: Princeton University Press.

Mazzarella, William. 2003. *Shoveling Smoke: Advertising and Globalization in Contemporary India.* Durham: Duke University Press.

McCloskey, Donald. 1985. *The Rhetoric of Economics.* Madison: University of Wisconsin Press.

Merry, Sally Engle. 2005. "Anthropology and Activism: Researching Human Rights Across Porous Boundaries." *Political and Legal Anthropology Review* 28:240–57.

———. 2006a. "Anthropology and International Law." *Annual Review of Anthropology* 35:99–116.

———. 2006b. *Human Rights and Gender Violence: Translating International Law into Local Justice.* Chicago: University of Chicago Press.

———. 2008. "International Law and Sociolegal Scholarship: Toward a Spatial Global Legal Pluralism." *Studies in Law, Politics, and Society* 41:149–68.

———. 2011. "Measuring the World: Indicators, Human Rights, and Global Governance." *Current Anthropology* 52(3):S83–S95.

Miller, Peter, and Nikolas Rose. 2008. *Governing the Present: Administering Economic, Social and Personal Life.* Cambridge, UK: Polity Press.

Minow, Martha. 2003. "Public and Private Partnerships: Accounting for the New Religion." *Harvard Law Review* 116:1229–70.

Morgan, Bronwen. 2003. "The Economisation of Politics: Metaregulation as a Form of Nonjudicial Legality." *Social and Legal Studies* 12:489–523.

Mosse, David. 2004a. "Is Good Policy Unimplementable? Reflections on the Ethnography of Aid Policy and Practice." *Development and Change* 35:639–71.

———. 2004b. "Social Analysis as Product Development: Anthropologists at Work in the World Bank." In *The Development of Religion, The Religion of Development,* edited by Ananta Kumar Giri et al., 77–87. Amsterdam: Eburon Delft.

———. 2005. "Global Governance and the Ethnography of International Aid." In *The Aid Effect: Giving and Governing in International Development,* edited by David Mosse and David Lewis, 1–36. London: Pluto Press.

Nielson, Daniel L., and Michael J. Tierney. 2003. "Delegation to International Organizations: Agency Theory and World Bank Environmental Reform." *International Organization* 57:241–76.

Norton, Joseph J. 2001. "International Financial Institutions and the Movement Toward Greater Accountability and Transparency: The Case of Legal Reform Pro-
grammes and the Problem of Evaluation." *International Lawyer* 35:1443–74.

Pahuja, Sundhya. 2007. "Rights as Regulation: The Integration of Development and
Human Rights." In *The Intersection of Rights and Regulation: New Directions
in Sociolegal Scholarship*, edited by Bronwen Morgan, 167–91. Aldershot, UK:
Ashgate.

Palacio, Ana. 2006. "The Way Forward: Human Rights and the World Bank." *Development Outreach*. http://siteresources.worldbank.org/EXTSITETOOLS/
Resources/PalacioDevtOutreach.pdf (last accessed on Dec. 5, 2011).

Parajuli, Pramod. 1991. "Power and Knowledge in Development Discourse." *International Social Science Journal* 127:173–90.

Pascale, Richard T. 1985. "The Paradox of 'Corporate Culture': Reconciling Ourselves to Socialization." *California Management Review* 27:26–41.

Payer, Cheryl. 1982. *The World Bank: A Critical Analysis*. New York: Monthly Review
Press.

Pettit, Philip. 1989. "Consequentialism and Respect for Persons." *Ethics* 100:116–26.

Pfeffer, Jeffrey. 1981. *Power in Organizations*. Marshfield, MA: Pitman.

———. 1997. *New Directions for Organization Theory: Problems and Prospects*. New
York: Oxford University Press.

Pildes, Richard H., and Cass R. Sunstein. 1995. "Reinventing the Regulatory State."
University of Chicago Law Review 62:1–129.

Piron, Laure-Hélène, and Tammie O'Neil. 2006. *Integrating Human Rights into Development: A Synthesis of Donor Approaches and Experiences*. Paris: Organization for Economic Cooperation and Development (OECD).

Polzer, Tara. 2001. "Corruption: Deconstructing the World Bank Discourse." Development Studies Institute Working Paper Series No. 01-18. London School of
Economics.

Porter, Theodore M. 1995. *Trust in Numbers: The Pursuit of Objectivity in Science and
Public Life*. Princeton, NJ: Princeton University Press.

Power, Michael. 1997. *The Audit Society: Rituals of Verification*. Oxford: Oxford University Press.

———. 2004. *The Risk Management of Everything: Rethinking the Politics of Uncertainty*. London: Demos.

———. 2007. *Organized Uncertainty: Designing a World of Risk Management*. Oxford: Oxford University Press.

Price, David. 1989. *Before the Bulldozer: The Nambiquara Indians and the World
Bank*. Cabin John, MD: Seven Locks Press.

Rajagopal, Balakrishnan. 2003. *International Law from Below: Development, Social*

Movements and Third World Resistance. Cambridge, UK: Cambridge University Press.

————. 2007. "Introduction: Encountering Ambivalence." In *The Practice of Human Rights: Tracking Law Between the Global and the Local*, edited by Mark Goodale and Sally Engle Merry, 273–84. Cambridge, UK: Cambridge University Press.

Ratner, Steven R. 2001. "Corporations and Human Rights: A Theory of Legal Responsibility." *Yale Law Journal* 111:443–545.

Rigo, Andres. 1997. "Roundtable of International Financial Institutions General Counsels." *American Society of International Law Proceedings* 91:199–200.

Riles, Annelise. 2006. "Skepticism, Intimacy and the Ethnographic Subject: Human Rights as Legal Knowledge." *American Anthropologist* 108:52–65.

Rose, Nikolas. 1999. *Powers of Freedom: Reframing Political Thought*. Cambridge: Cambridge University Press.

Rosenthal, Debra. 1990. *At the Heart of the Bomb: The Deadly Allure of Weapons Work*. Reading, MA: Addison-Wesley.

Royo, Antoinette G. 1998. "The Philippines: Against the People's Wishes, the Mt. Apo Story." In *The Struggle for Accountability: The World Bank, NGOs, and Grassroots Movements*, edited by Jonathan A. Fox and L. David Brown, 151–79. Cambridge, MA: MIT Press.

Ruggie, John Gerard. 1998. "What Makes the World Hang Together: Neo-Utilitarianism and the Social Constructivist Challenge." *International Organization* 52:855–85.

Santos, Alvaro. 2006. "The World Bank's Uses of the 'Rule of Law' Promise in Economic Development." In *The New Law and Economic Development*, edited by David Trubek and Alvaro Santos, 253–300. New York: Cambridge University Press.

Sarat, Austin, and Thomas R. Kearns. 2001. "The Unsettled Status of Human Rights: An Introduction." In *Human Rights: Concepts, Contests, Contingencies*, edited by Austin Sarat and Thomas R. Kearns, 1–24. Ann Arbor: University of Michigan Press.

Sarooshi, Dan. 2005. *International Organizations and Their Exercise of Sovereign Powers*. Oxford: Oxford University Press.

Schein, Edgar H. 1991. "What Is Culture?" In *Reframing Organizational Culture*, edited by Peter J. Frost et al., 243–53. London: Sage.

Schermers, H. G. 1998. "The Legal Bases of International Organization Action." In *A Handbook on International Organizations*, edited by René-Jean Dupuy, 401–11. Boston: Nijhoff.

Scott, James C. 1998. *Seeing Like a State: How Certain Schemes to Improve the Human Condition Have Failed*. New Haven, CT: Yale University Press.

Sen, Amartya. 2004. "Elements of a Theory of Human Rights." *Philosophy & Public Affairs* 32:315–56.

———. 2006. "Human Rights and the Limits of Law." *Cardozo Law Review* 27:2913–27.

Sevastopulo, Demetri. Nov. 3, 2003. "World Bank Arm May Add Human Rights to Its Criteria." *Financial Times*.

Shamir, Ronen. 2004. "The De-Radicalization of Corporate Social Responsibility." *Critical Sociology* 30:1–21.

———. 2010. "Capitalism, Governance, and Authority: The Case of Corporate Social Responsibility." *Annual Review of Law and Social Science* 6:1–23.

Shihata, Ibrahim. 1988. "The World Bank and Human Rights: An Analysis of the Legal Issues and the Record of Achievements." *Denver Journal of International Law and Policy* 17:39–66.

———. 1991a. *The World Bank in a Changing World: Selected Essays.* Hague: Martinus Nijhoff.

———. 1991b. *The World Bank in a Changing World: Volume I.* Boston: Martinus Nijhoff.

———. 1995. *The World Bank in a Changing World: Volume II.* Boston: Martinus Nijhoff.

———. 1997. "Role of the World Bank's General Counsel." *American Society of International Law Proceedings* 91:214–22.

———. 2000a. *The World Bank in a Changing World: Volume III.* Boston: Martinus Nijhoff.

———. 2000b. *The World Bank Legal Papers.* Hague: Martinus Nijhoff.

Shore, Cris, and Susan Wright. 2000. "Coercive Accountability: The Rise of Audit Culture in Higher Education." In *Audit Cultures: Anthropological Studies in Accountability, Ethics and the Academy,* edited by Marilyn Strathern, 57–89. London: Routledge.

Simmel, Georg. 1978 (1907). *The Philosophy of Money,* edited by David Frisby. London: Routledge & Kegan Paul.

Skogly, Sigrun I. 2001. *The Human Rights Obligations of the World Bank and the International Monetary Fund.* London: Cavendish.

Snow, David A., and Robert D. Benford. 1992. "Master Frames and Cycles of Protest." In *Frontiers in Social Movement Theory,* edited by Aldon Morris and Carol McClurg Mueller, 133–55. New Haven: Yale University Press.

Snyder, Francis. 1999. "Governing Economic Globalization: Global Legal Pluralism and European Law." *European Law Journal* 5:334–74.

Stiglitz, Joseph E. 1999. "The World Bank at the Millennium." *Economic Journal* 109:F577–F597.

Strang, David, and Dong-Il Jung. 2005. "Organizational Change as an Orchestrated

Social Movement: Recruitment to a Corporate Quality Initiative." In *Social Movements and Organization Theory*, edited by Gerald F. Davis et al., 280–309. New York: Cambridge University Press.

Strathern, Marilyn, ed. 2000. *Audit Cultures: Anthropological Studies in Accountability, Ethics, and the Academy*. London and New York: Routledge.

Sunstein, Cass R. 2002. *The Cost-Benefit State: The Future of Regulatory Protection*. Chicago: American Bar Association.

Treakle, Kay. 1998. "Ecuador: Structural Adjustment and Indigenous and Environmentalist Resistance." In *The Struggle for Accountability: The World Bank, NGOs, and Grassroots Movements*, edited by Jonathan A. Fox and L. David Brown, 219–64. Cambridge, MA: MIT Press.

Trubek, David, and Alvaro Santos, eds. 2006. *The New Law and Economic Development*. New York: Cambridge University Press.

United Nations Development Programme (UNDP). 2005. "Human Rights in UNDP Practice Note." http://www.undp.org/governance/docs/HRPN_English.pdf (last accessed Dec. 6, 2011).

Uvin, Peter. 2004. *Human Rights and Development*. Bloomfield, CT: Kumarian Press.

———. 2007. "From the Right to Development to the Rights-Based Approach: How 'Human Rights' Entered Development." *Development in Practice* 17:597–606.

Van Maanen, John, and Stephen Barley. 1985. "Cultural Organization: Fragments of a Theory." In *Organization Culture*, edited by Peter J. Frost et al., 31–54. Beverly Hills, CA: Sage.

Wade, Robert. 1997. "Greening the Bank: The Struggle over the Environment, 1970–1995." In *The World Bank: Its First Half Century* (vol. 1), edited by Devesh Kapur et al., 611–734. Washington, DC: Brookings Institution.

Wallace, Tina. 2003. "NGO Dilemmas: Trojan Horses for Global Neoliberalism?" In *Socialist Register 2004: The New Imperial Challenge*, edited by Leo Panitch and Colin Leys, 202–19. London: Merlin Press.

Waltz, Kenneth N. 1979. *Theory of International Politics*. Reading, MA: Addison-Wesley.

Warren, Kay. 2007. "The 2000 UN Human Trafficking Protocol: Rights, Enforcement, Vulnerabilities." In *The Practice of Human Rights: Tracking Law Between the Global and the Local*, edited by Mark Goodale and Sally Engle Merry, 242–69. Cambridge, UK: Cambridge University Press.

Weaver, Catherine. 2008. *Hypocrisy Trap: The World Bank and the Poverty of Reform*. Princeton, NJ: Princeton University Press.

Weber, Max. 1948. *From Max Weber: Essays in Sociology*. Edited by Hans Gerth and C. Wright Mills. London: Routledge.

———. 1978. *Economy and Society: An Outline of Interpretive Sociology.* Edited by Guenther Roth and Claus Wittich. Berkeley: University of California Press.

Weiss, Edith Brown, and Harold K. Jacobson, eds. 1998. *Engaging Countries: Strengthening Compliance with International Environmental Accords.* Cambridge, MA: MIT Press.

Weissbrodt, David, and Muria Kruger. 2003. "Norms on the Responsibilities of Transnational Corporations and Other Business Enterprises with Regard to Human Rights." *American Journal of International Law* 97:901–22.

Wendt, Alexander. 1992. "Anarchy Is What States Make of It: The Social Construction of Power Politics." *International Organization* 46:391–425.

Wilson, James Q. 1989. *Bureaucracy: What Government Agencies Do and Why They Do It.* New York: Basic Books.

Wilson, Richard A. 2001. *The Politics of Truth and Reconciliation in South Africa: Legitimizing the Post-Apartheid State.* Cambridge, UK: Cambridge University Press.

———. 2006a. "Is the Legalization of Human Rights Really the Problem? Genocide in the Guatemalan Historical Clarification Commission." In *The Legalization of Human Rights: Multidisciplinary Perspectives on Human Rights and Human Rights Law,* edited by Saladin Meckled-Garcia and Basak Çali, 81–98. Abingdon, UK: Routledge.

———. 2007. "Tyrannosaurus Lex: The Anthropology of Human Rights and Transnational Law." In *The Practice of Human Rights: Tracking Law Between the Global and the Local,* edited by Mark Goodale and Sally Engle Merry, 342–69. Cambridge, UK. Cambridge University Press.

Wolfensohn, James. 2000. "Transcript of NGO Meeting with Mr. Wolfensohn," Prague, 22 September 2000. http://www.worldbank.org.md/WBSITE/EXTERNAL/COUNTRIES/ECAEXT/MOLDOVAEXTN/0,,print:YisCURL:YcontentMDK:20025788menuPK:34478pagePK:34370piPK:34424theSitePK:302251,00.html (last accessed Dec. 6, 2011).

Woods, Ngaire. 2006. *The Globalizers: The IMF, the World Bank, and the Their Borrowers.* Ithaca, NY: Cornell University Press.

World Bank. 1989. *Sub-Saharan Africa: From Crisis to Sustainable Growth. A Long-Term Perspective Study.* Washington, DC: World Bank.

———. 1997. *Helping Countries Combat Corruption: Progress at the World Bank Since 1997.* Washington, DC: World Bank.

———. 1998. *Development and Human Rights: The Role of the World Bank.* Washington, DC: World Bank.

———. 1999. *Principles and Good Practice in Social Policy: Issues and Areas for Public Action.* Washington, DC: World Bank.

————. 2001. *Task Force on the World Bank Group and Middle Income Countries: Final Report*. Washington, DC: World Bank.

————. 2004. *An OED Review of Social Development in Bank Activities*. Washington, DC: World Bank.

————. 2005. *Empowering People by Transforming Institutions: Social Development in World Bank Operations*. Washington, DC: World Bank.

————. 2006. *World Development Report*. Washington, DC: World Bank.

Wright, Susan. 1994. "'Culture' in Anthropology and Organization Studies." In *Anthropology of Organizations*, edited by Susan Wright, 1–31. London: Routledge.

Zaloom, Caitlin. 2006. *Out of the Pits: Traders and Technology from Chicago to London*. Chicago: University of Chicago Press.

Index

Judging War, Judging History: Behind Truth and Reconciliation
Pierre Hazan
2010

Localizing Transitional Justice:
Interventions and Priorities after Mass Violence
Edited by Rosalind Shaw and Lars Waldorf, with Pierre Hazan
2010

Surrendering to Utopia: An Anthropology of Human Rights
Mark Goodale
2009

Human Rights Matters: Local Politics and National Human Rights Institutions
Julie A. Mertus
2009

Human Rights for the 21st Century: Sovereignty, Civil Society, Culture
Helen M. Stacy
2009